CONTRARY OPINION

T0367742

Wiley Trading Advantage

CONTRARY OPINION

Using Sentiment to Profit in the Futures Markets

R. Earl Hadady

John Wiley & Sons, Inc.

New York • Chichester • Weinheim • Brisbane • Singapore • Toronto

This book is printed on acid-free paper. ∞

Copyright © 2000 by R. Earl Hadady. All rights reserved.

Published by John Wiley & Sons, Inc.

Published simultaneously in Canada.

This publication is designed to provide accurate and authoritative information in regard to the subject matter covered. It is sold with the understanding that the pub-lisher is not engaged in rendering professional services. If professional advice or other expert assistance is required, the services of a competent professional person should be sought.

Library of Congress Cataloging-in-Publication Data:

Hadady, R. Earl (Robert Earl), 1920–
    Contrary opinion : using sentiment to profit in the futures markets / R. Earl Hadady.
        p.   cm. — (Wiley trading advantage)
    Includes bibliographical references and index.
    ISBN 0–471–36353–7 (cloth : alk. paper)
    1. Futures.   2. Investment analysis.   I. Title.   II. Series.
HG6024.H33   2000
33.64'5—dc21   99–38493

10 9 8 7 6 5 4 3 2 1

CONTENTS

List of Figures and Charts

LIST OF FIGURES AND CHARTS

Figures

Charts

Contrary Opinion

PREFACE

The conventional wisdom in books, articles, and other material typically depicts the futures markets as a tug of war between supply and demand. In concept, the futures markets appear to be straightforward and simple. But make no mistake about it: Nothing could be farther from the truth. Perhaps there is no other subject covered by so much misinformation, which represents an almost certain prescription for failure. Otherwise, why would so many lose? Estimates of the number of participants who lose range from around 75 percent to as high as 95 percent. There are two basic reasons why so many fail to succeed.

First, the markets' apparent simplicity is very deceptive. The purpose of this book is to strip away the cloak of misinformation and bring into sharp focus the principles involved. It is a self-evident truth that you can't consistently win in futures, checkers, chess, or whatever until you know how the game is really played.

Second, the futures markets act like a magnet to people who like action. Many want to have positions in the markets all the time, but low-risk, high-profit trades only occur infrequently in a given futures—the trades that make you a winner over the long haul. Hence, the typical personality of many who enter the markets works against them. Patience is a vital characteristic of the long-term, successful trader.

Now, let's learn how the game is really played and what *Contrary Opinion* is all about. I hope you'll find my informal, down-home writing style easy reading as well as informative.

R. Earl Hadady
October 25, 1999

ACKNOWLEDGMENTS

The author wishes to express appreciation to Richard Ishida, Editor of the *Bullish Consensus*, for taking the time to read the manuscript and provide his comments. He is also responsible for all of the price/consensus charts included in the last chapter of this book.

CONTRARY OPINION

Chapter 1

LITTLE-KNOWN FACTS

*The obvious is that which is never seen until someone
expresses it simply.*

— Kahlil Gibran

This book is written for both the experienced trader and the
person new to the futures markets. Many of the ideas and
much of the information expressed in this book are at odds
with conventional market wisdom, which has shown itself
to be of little value. The validity of this statement is borne
out by the fact that the majority of market participants lose.
Your broker will readily confirm this last statement. If both
the conventional market wisdom and printed material on
the market were correct, the balance between winners and
losers would be more nearly equal. This text may be especially helpful and make the going easier for a new trader,
who will not be encumbered by prior ideas and information.

1

Is the Logical Approach Illogical?

Most new market participants approach the financial markets with the idea that a logical and systematic approach will make them winners. They believe all they have to do is study, become knowledgeable, do their homework, utilize a computer, and profits will roll in. After all, isn't that what all of the promotional mail that you get keeps telling you? Some even offer a sure-fire way of beating a particular market. Simply send $X and you'll receive the WHIZ system of investing or trading that will make you wealthy in just a few years.

As any trading advisor and trader can tell you, this just isn't so. Actually, most people who enter these markets lose. Hard numbers on the percentage of investors who turn up losers is not available, but when your broker tells you it is so, and he's selling it, you know it is true. It is a generally accepted fact that probably 75 to 90 percent of the speculators who enter the futures markets lose. Estimates for the stock market are undoubtedly less discouraging, but trading volume on the exchanges attributed to individual investors has steadily given way to the fund managers. This is an indication that over the long haul investors as a whole tend to lose and hence seek professional management of their funds. Depending on the time span and the market during that period, professional management is a mixed bag. Almost anyone can make money in a bull market, one that is steadily moving higher, whereas in a bear market, most of the funds turn in losing records.

Since most of the market participants are probably above average in intelligence and they are losers, it is logical to assume that the books and material they have used to develop their trading expertise must be misleading and/or wrong.

Dissimilarities between the Futures and Stock Markets

Most new market participants think the futures markets and the stock market are very similar. It is important to recognize, however, that the stock market and the futures markets are structured differently and that an appropriate and winning strategy for one market will not necessarily produce profits in the other market. A game is defined as "a situation that involves rivalry between opposing interests with the object of maximizing their wins and minimizing their losses in a given time period." Based on this definition, then, the futures market is a game, but the stock market is not.

1. In the stock market, theoretically every investor can be a winner and there is no time limit.

2. A futures market is a zero-sum game; that is, the money lost by some speculators and hedgers is exactly equal to the money won by other speculators and hedgers. Note that this statement does not mean there is a trader who wins for every trader who loses. Moreover, the game ends for a given contract on a preset expiration date.

In the stock market, everyone who trades a particular stock can be a winner. For example, on the initial public offering, an investor purchases stock in the ABC Company. The company prospers, earnings increase, and the price of its stock rises. The investor sells the stock and makes a profit. The company continues to prosper, earnings rise, and its stock price moves higher. The second investor sells his stock and takes a profit. If the company continues to prosper, this buying and selling sequence can continue an indefinite number of times, with each investor making a profit on his sale. Effectively, both the company and its stockholders are on the same side of the market. As the company's intrinsic value increases, shares in its owner-ship, represented by stock, likewise increase.

The preceding scenario isn't possible in the futures market where you have traders on opposite sides of the market. One group of traders anticipates a decrease in the market value of the commodity and the other group an increase. Moreover, trading of a given futures contract is limited to a specific time period, at the end of which all positions must be liquidated and settled. In short, it is a zero-sum game in which some traders must lose for others to win.

Are There Only Two Basic Ways to Analyze the Market?

Most market participants think there are only two basic ways to analyze the futures markets—fundamental or technical.

Fundamental analysis refers to the factors involving sup-ply and demand for a given commodity in the real world.

For example, the fundamentals for soybeans would involve the current stock of soybeans, the condition of the new crop in the field, the growing environment for the new crop, the present consumption rate, and a myriad of other factors. Typically, it is a full-time occupation for one person to be on top of the fundamentals for just a single commodity.

Technical analysis refers to data related to the current price, such as the price trend and trading volume. Traders who use technical analysis as the basis for trading generally assume that all fundamental factors are reflected in the day-to-day prices and their parameters.

But there is a third way, not related to the other two—sentiment analysis. Sentiment analysis is a determination of the percentage of market participants who are bullish, neutral, or bearish. Market sentiment is determined by polling and is expressed as the number of traders who are bullish or bearish on a given market at some specific time. As an example, if the sentiment for gold on June 15 is stated as a Bullish Consensus of 60 percent, it means that 6 out of 10 (60 percent) of the traders in gold are bullish and are expecting prices to rise. The remaining 40 percent are either neutral or bearish. Sentiment analysis can be likened to a preelection poll in which voters are asked how they are going to cast their vote. In a market sentiment poll, the reason for a market participant's bullish, neutral, or bearish stance is of no consequence. Hence, it is unrelated to fundamental or technical analysis. Sentiment analysis is the principal subject of this book. Chapter 10 provides a number of charts that illustrate the relationship between sentiment and prices, and how this information can be used to trade for profit.

Trading Activity Parameters

Most market participants think the futures markets have only three basic parameters—price, volume, and open interest. Actually, there are five. The other two are market sentiment and market composition. As suggested earlier, *market sentiment* refers to the percentage of traders in the market who are bullish, bearish, or neutral. *Market composition* refers to the percentage of futures contracts held by large traders, hedgers, and small traders. Composition classifications are defined by the Commodity Futures Trading Commission, the government agency that regulates these markets. Later chapters of this book deal with market sentiment and composition in detail.

Trading Parameters
Price
Volume
Open Interest
Market Sentiment
Market Composition

Do You Have a 50/50 Chance of Winning?

Most market participants think they have a 50/50 chance of winning because the market can only go up or down, since sideways doesn't make them either winners or losers.

Little-Known Facts

Consider the following: for a futures trader to be a winner using fundamental and/or technical analysis of a market, these conditions must be satisfied:

1. An analysis must correctly foretell the direction of a significant move in the market.
2. A position must be taken in the market before the forecast develops; otherwise the position is taken too late.
3. A large unfavorable price move *must not* occur before the forecast develops; otherwise, the position is likely to be abandoned with a loss, before it turns profitable.
4. After a position is taken, the majority of market participants must take similar positions, for whatever reasons, in order to power the market in the forecasted direction.

The probability is not very high that these four events will occur in the required sequence. Indeed, on a random basis, it is only one in eight. Thus, it is easy to see why futures trading generally involves considerable risk.

Stated another way, a trader using either fundamental or technical analysis must anticipate what the other traders are going to do, regardless of whether they are right or wrong, and must be ahead of them. It is important not to confuse (a) where one's analysis predicts the market should go, which is unimportant, with (b) where the majority of the market participants thinks the market is headed, which is important. Anticipating what the crowd will do is an iffy business. A remark by the former chairman of the New York Mercantile Exchange, Michael D. Marks, succinctly sums up the increasing importance of market sentiment. "As factual information becomes harder to obtain and verify, and as the quantity increases, opinions will become more important. That is, `don't tell me what the facts are, rather, tell me what everyone thinks they are'."

Traders who use fundamental analysis would argue that real-world fundamentals eventually become generally known and determine the market price. This has been a passport to disaster in some notable cases. The 1976–1977 Cook–Hunt soybean market debacle, described in some detail in the next chapter, is a case in point.

Analyzing Winners versus Losers

Many market participants haven't grasped what the high percentage of losers in the futures markets really means. The following simple mathematics can provide an important insight. Since there is a winning contract for every losing contract, here is what the ratio of winners to losers shows. Letting:

T = Total number of traders in the market

N_L = Average number of contracts (long and short) held by losers

N_W = Average number of contracts (long and short) held by winners

For the situation where 80 percent of the traders lose, the relationship is therefore:

8

Little-Known Facts

80% $T \times N_L$ = Total number of all outstanding contracts (long and short) held by losers

20% $T \times N_W$ = Total number of all outstanding contracts (long and short) held by winners

In reviewing these equations, it would seem improper to combine the longs and shorts held by either the losers or the winners. It would seem that one side or the other must win; that is, if the longs turned out to be winners, the shorts would be losers. But this is not the case. Market positions, both long and short, are taken at different times and prices. One buyer may be a winner because he or she bought at a low prices, whereas another buyer, who bought at a much higher price, could be a loser. Furthermore, the market is so volatile that underfinanced longs and shorts can be blown out before prices move far enough in one direction to produce a profit for them. Even the best traders in the business rarely have more than 50 percent winning trades.

Since the total number of winning contracts to losing contracts must be exactly equal, the following statement has to be true:

$$80\% \ T \times N_L = 20\% \ T \times N_W$$

Thus, in this case where 80 percent of the traders lose:

$$N_L = \frac{20\% \ T \times N_W}{80\% T} = \frac{1}{4} N_W$$

In other words, the average trader who loses holds only one-fourth as many contracts as the average winner. The

9

following tabuation shows the average number of contracts held by winners for various ratios of winners to
losers:

Speculators Who Lose	Average Number of Contracts Held by Winners vs. Losers
75%	3 times
80%	4 times
85%	5.6 times
90%	9 times
95%	19 times

In short, the average winning trader holds more contracts than the average losing trader because there are
fewer winning traders than losing traders. This becomes
clear when you begin to analyze the futures market and
get its workings clearly in focus. And what is the significance? Since the exchanges and the brokerage houses
require margin money for each contract a speculator
holds, one who holds a lot of contracts clearly has to be
better financed than a speculator who holds only a few.
Moreover, it means that the losses of the many participants
add up to a large gain for a relatively few traders.

The Word from the Futures Pit

On the floor of the exchanges it is not uncommon to hear
the expression, "The public is almost always wrong."
Hence, the local traders on the floor are usually eager to
take the other side of a trade for most orders entering the

pit from public speculators across the country. They are indeed right but for the wrong reason. A more correct expression would be, "The public almost always runs out of money before we do."

Here is an interesting example of "almost always." The Hunt silver debacle that occurred in late 1979 and early 1980 was one of those "almost but not always" exceptions. The public and Bunker Hunt kept buying silver until the exchange members, local floor traders and commercials, who were selling, began running out of money. When the situation got to the point where this group was in financial jeopardy, the little-known optional exchange rule of "liquidation only, no new positions" was invoked. Even with this rule, however, the shorts would have been killed had Bunker Hunt and the other longs been able to come up with enough money to accept delivery on all of the contracts they were holding. Since this was not the case, however, the longs had to deal with the shorts on terms dictated by the shorts. Paul Sarnoff's informative and enjoyable book, *Silver Bulls*, provides semifictional insights into the complete goings-on.

Some traders fail to appreciate the fact that in order for them to take a long or short position in the market, someone must take the other side of the trade. Thus, every time you buy, another trader or other traders must be willing to sell. In most cases, a floor trader, who is delighted to accommodate you, will take the other side of your order. Typically, the floor traders, the so-called locals, in the pit descend like a cloud of locusts on "order fillers" who execute buy and sell orders for off-the-floor traders. Since local traders on the floor do not pay commissions, they are willing to trade for small profits. They may initiate and offset trades literally within seconds, and they may become bullish or bearish on a commodity's prospects in an equally short period of time. Since short-term, small profits are their goal, they cannot afford to give up what is called the "edge" when trading.

Except in unusual cases, there is always a *bid* and *ask* price in the pit. Traders in the pit are willing either to buy or to sell at these prices. The difference between these two prices is called the *spread*. Some local floor traders may be willing either to buy at the bid price or to sell at the ask price. This type of trader is known as a *scalper*, and he may be in and out of the market 50 or more times during a trading day. He trades many times for very small profits, and the spread in most cases represents his profit. As a trader outside the exchange, you invariably have to give up the *edge* to someone on the floor each time you have an order executed.

Ideally, a scalper would like to be fully hedged by holding an equal number of short and long positions, thus eliminating concern as to whether prices are rising or declining. A scalper would also like to have acquired the long positions (bought) at the low end of the spread in prices, bid versus ask, and the short positions (sold) at the high end of the spread. Effectively, a scalper is buying "low" and selling "high."

The preceding "ideal" conditions are rarely available to the scalper, however, and his is a risky business. The risk increases in proportion to how fast prices are changing and the number of contracts that are changing hands. In a slow market, the spread is likely to be quite small. In a market where prices are increasing or decreasing rapidly and the volume is high, the spread will be large.

Little-Known Facts

Floor traders recognize the market for what it is: a money game in which knowledge of the commodity or security has little to do with making a profit. Many traders in the soybean pit couldn't differentiate between a soybean and a jelly bean, but it doesn't handicap them one bit when it comes to consistently making money off of outside speculators. Because floor traders are so quick to switch from being long to short in the market, artificial price turbulence is often created, one far removed from the underlying conditions of supply and demand. As a result, all but the strongest hands are often shaken out of the market by these random moves in prices. Floor traders, being realistic, do not argue with a market that is moving one way or the other. When the market moves against them, they are quick to accept losses in order to preserve their capital. Learning to understand the randomness of the marketplace is an essential part of futures trading.

Chapter 2

WORKINGS OF THE FUTURES MARKETS

The facts are unimportant! It's what they are perceived to be that determines the course of events.

— R. Earl Hadady

The need of producers and processors of commodities to minimize their risks in selling and buying commodities used in their businesses led to the establishment of *commodity markets.* Commodity markets first attained a degree of formalization—that is, a fixed time and place for trading—in ancient Greco-Roman times. In the United States, the first centralized commodity markets developed in New York in the 1700s, but they were largely cash markets. The first forward delivery market, that is, futures market, took place shortly after the founding of Chicago in 1833. In 1848 the first formal exchange, the Chicago Board of Trade, came into being.

For survival, producers of commodities such as corn, cattle, and sugar need to be assured of a fair price for their commodity at about the time they commit themselves to producing it, which is months before it is ready for market. In order to plan and price the final product, processors need to know in advance that they are going to be able to buy a given commodity at a specific price. Futures markets satisfy the needs of both the producers and processors to minimize their risks. The risk is transferred to people who want to speculate. Producers and processors of a given commodity who enter the market for the sole purpose of establishing a product's selling price and buying price at a future date are known as *hedgers*. In short, futures markets were established for the hedgers.

In recent years the trading of stock indexes, foreign currencies, bonds, and so on, for future delivery and in a manner similar to the original commodity markets, led to all of these markets being referred to as *futures markets*.

The majority of the participants in the futures markets engage in trading strictly for speculation, and so they have no intention of either delivering or accepting the commodity or security specified in the contract. In many instances, contracts are bought and sold a number of times during a given day. Holding a position over a couple of weeks is considered long term in the futures markets.

How Hedging Works

As just explained producers and processors who enter the futures market that involves the product they produce or process are called hedgers. Restated, a hedger is a market participant who wants to protect against the possibility of an adverse price move in a commodity or security.

16

An example of a hedger is a corn farmer who anticipates harvesting X bushels of corn several months in the future. The time is late July, and the current price of corn is higher than it was in prior months. If the farmer could sell his corn today, rather than in late October when he will actually be harvesting it, he would be assured of a significant profit. Such a sale could be made in July in the futures market using the December corn contract on the Chicago Board of Trade. Once the sale is made in the futures market, the corn farmer has established the price that he will get for his corn and he will care less what the price is in October, when he actually harvests it.

Much of the time, the hedgers are in reality speculating. Besides the problems of predicting the final size of their crops, and the like, hedgers are not immune to speculative fever. Some candid conversations with a few so-called hedgers will quickly dispel the storybook idea that they simply take positions to offset their future needs. On the production side, hedgers typically include farmers and growers, cattlemen, hog raisers, lumber mills, metal mining companies, and oil producers. On the processing side, hedgers include food processing companies, meatpackers, textile mills, construction companies, and oil refiners,

The Futures Game

Even hedgers and speculators who have been in the markets for years sometimes fail to appreciate the differences between the stock and futures markets. In the futures markets, the total profits are exactly equal to the total losses, so some traders are going to win and some are going to lose. Of all the money games, the futures markets are perhaps the most specifically structured of any. Here is the framework:

1. A buyer and seller are required for each transaction.
2. Each transaction involves two contracts:
   a. Long contract—acquired by a trader who believes prices will be higher in the future; this trader is referred to as a *bull*.
   b. Short contract—acquired by a trader who believes prices will be lower in the future; this trader is referred to as a *bear*.
3. For every winning contract there is a losing contract. It is a zero-sum game.
4. There is no limit on the number of contracts; that is, the number of contracts is not limited to the deliverable supply of the commodity or security.
5. Contracts have a specific expiration date, on or before which they must be settled.
6. The typical money (margin) that one must deposit to buy or sell a contract is usually less than 10 percent of the actual value of the contract. There is extremely high leverage in trading futures; for example, the margin requirement to trade 100 ounces of gold with a price of say $300 per ounce (contract value $30,000) is typically about $1,500, a leverage of 20 to 1.

One key reason why the futures game is so attractive is the winner to loser relationship. Rid yourself of the idea that there is a winner for every loser and vice versa.

Rather, there is a winning contract for every losing contract, which is significantly different. Since some 75 percent or more speculators lose trading futures, the losses of many become the profits of a few.

Conventional Wisdom Must be Wrong

Because so many speculators in the futures markets end up losing, there is a constant turnover of participants. This reveals an important attribute of these markets. If the conventional wisdom found in current literature were correct and provided a good model of the market, why would so many speculators lose? Certainly the balance would be closer to 50/50 rather than around 80/20 that knowledgeable people estimate.

Most speculators who lose turn to the literature or advisors thinking that they must be doing something wrong and there has to be a better way. Yet the majority continue to lose. This is certainly indicative that conventional wisdom, if not totally wrong, must be sadly incomplete. In short, speculators have almost universally found that conventional wisdom on the futures market is a sure prescription for *how* to lose!

You Can Be Right about the Fundamentals and Still Lose

Here is a classic and true story about how you can be right about the fundamentals and still lose. For the soybean crop year of 1976–1977, the analysts at Cook Industries had evaluated the fundamentals and determined that an adequate supply of beans would be available through September when harvesting of the new crop would begin. However, in the spring of 1976 the prices of soybean futures, traded on the Chicago Board of Trade, continued to rise. This was an indication that most market participants believed there was going to be a shortage of beans before the new crop became available in October. Based on Cook's analysis that there would be an adequate supply of beans until the new beans were harvested, they were an aggressive seller in the futures market, although prices continued to rise. Unfortunately for Cook, Bunker Hunt and family were buying soybean futures. On June 1, Cook Industries, a publicly held company, issued a news release that their losses were "likely to be in excess of $60 million" as a result of having to cover (exit) their short positions in the soybean futures market.

As it turned out, Cook's analysis had evaluated the market correctly. There was an adequate supply of soybeans, and prices tumbled before harvest time— unfortunately, too late to save Cook Industries from having to liquidate much of its assets and barely escape bankruptcy.

You may be thinking, "but that is just an example of a mistaken supply–demand estimate on the part of the bulls in this case." If this is what you are thinking, these subtle points have escaped you:

1. You can lose even when your analysis of the fundamentals, the supply and demand factors, is correct. In

fact, correctly evaluating the fundamentals is not related to winning.

2. You can be market right if you have enough money.

Summary of How the Futures Markets Work

1. The futures game is basically a money game—not a game involving the supply–demand of the underlying commodity or security as is commonly depicted.

2. Real-world supply and demand are not reflected in the day-to-day cash (commonly referred to as the spot) price, which is as speculative as futures prices. Both futures prices and the spot price fluctuate widely, and often wildly, around an imaginary and idealized price that represents a balance between supply and demand in the real world. Since most businesses plan and operate on a monthly basis, a 21-day (the average number of business days in a month) moving average of the daily cash price is believed to be commensurate with this idealized price for most commodities.

3. The contract side, long or short, with the fewest participants always wins in the end, because they are better financed; that is, they have more money.

4. Attempting to decipher the fundamentals, the supply and demand factors, is a complete waste of time for two reasons:

    a. Acquiring expertise in just a single commodity is a full-time, long-term occupation for an individual.

21

b. Even though you might be fortunate enough to have the right answers from time to time, there is no assurance that large money interests will not be on the opposite side and make your knowledge unprofitable (e.g., the Cook–Hunt soybean situation covered earlier).

5. Once a major price move gets underway, it feeds on its own momentum, because the winners have the advantage of being able to leverage additional positions (put up roughly only 10 percent of the value of the contract), whereas the losers must fully cover their losses, dollar for dollar.

6. When the market moves opposite to the apparent fundamentals, this is a tip-off as to which side of the market the major money interests are on. The Commodity Futures Trading Commission report, "Commitment of Traders in Futures," covered in Chapter 8, can help you here. Note that this may be short-term money positioning involving only a few days or a week or so.

7. A news event is *not required* to precipitate an explosive price move. Like an avalanche being started by a single falling rock, the decision of a single trader to exit the market when it is precariously balanced can produce a chain reaction and an explosive move.

8. The big money in the market is typically taking positions contrary to what is breaking in the news; that is, they're the idiots who are selling when the news is bullish. Remember that someone has to be selling if you're buying futures. And don't forget, in the end it's those "idiots" who end up winning and heading

for the bank. Therefore, you'll do well not to pay too much attention to the news. Isn't the situation always the most bullish at the top and most bearish at the bottom?

Can You Win?

The answer is yes, but, it "ain't" easy! Here are the basic requirements one must have:

1. A thorough knowledge of how the markets work.
2. Experience.
3. A suitable trading plan.
4. Appropriate strategies for entering and exiting the market and placing protective stop orders.
5. A good money management plan.
6. The psychological makeup that enables you to accept losses with equanimity. Even the most successful traders only bat about 50 percent; that is, about half of their trades are losers. Consequently, winning trades have to produce big profits, while losing trades must be limited to small losses.
7. Lots of money.

To make it really big, one must have the confidence to plunge in at that opportune time which occurs perhaps only once or twice a year. "Most commodity traders die broke" is an old saw that is so appropriate in this business. It seems that, sooner or later, all big commodity traders make the plunge and find themselves on the wrong side of the market. Perhaps the worst thing that can happen to a newly initiated futures trader is to start making money right away. It almost invariably leads to overconfidence followed by overtrading one's resources—it all seems so easy. Be wary. It's an invitation to disaster.

Analyzing the Markets So You Can Be a Winner

Although participants in a given market are quick to agree that price moves are the result of their actions, they often forget and lose sight of this basic and very important fact. Stated another way, the action of the participants is the *only* reason prices move! Participants buy and sell based on where they "think" prices are headed—which may or may not be in accord with the facts in the real world. However, if enough market participants believe the market is going to move higher and begin to position themselves accordingly, the market will move higher, regardless of what the real-world facts are, or vice versa.

Some very astute market analysts have been involved in forecasting over the last hundred years or so, but they have failed to fully recognize the significance of what the above paragraph implies. Their approach to deciphering the markets has always boiled down to either fundamental or technical analysis. In the futures markets, the fundamentals relate to all of the supply and demand factors, such as the number of bushels of the commodity produced, consumption, exports, and a myriad of other considerations. With respect to the other approach, technical tools simply deal with the parameters that are involved in the trading activity (i.e., the price, volume, etc.). The theory behind the technical approach is that all fundamental factors are automatically integrated into the price action, trading volume, and so on, of the futures being traded.

Most analysts tend to overlook a forecasting tool that directly deciphers the participants' activities, the real motive power in the market. In short, analysts have based their analysis on trying to decipher the participants' motivations. This is very chancy occupation at best and an indirect approach. The direct approach would be to simply poll the participants and find out what they plan to do and are doing.

Some Examples

The following examples may help to clarify and validate the power of using sentiment in trading:

Assume that you are in an auditorium filled with people and that this group constitutes everyone who trades XYZ. If you were able to poll these people and obtain their thoughts, would you need any other information to trade XYZ profitably? The answer of course is, "no." You can forget the conventional fundamental and technical tools used by the analysts. The price of XYZ will move in the direction as viewed by the majority, whether they be bullish or bearish, whether they be right or wrong, and for whatever reason, until essentially everyone is fully positioned. At that point, the fuel that powered the move has been exhausted, and we have a Contrary Opinion situation, which is covered later in this book. At this juncture, prices can move only one way, in the opposite direction.

Consider a preelection poll of voters. Polls have become so accurate that the results are generally accepted as gospel. The vital question in such polls is, "Who are you going to vote for?" The reasons for casting a vote for A rather than B is of secondary interest, and the rationale for the decision is typically not all that easy to define. Rather than being a yes/no, black/white type of answer, all kinds of subjective thinking may enter the picture. As so often occurs in news stories, the rationale given for an occurrence seems logical, but in actuality it may or may not have been the real underlying reason. In short, one's accuracy in forecasting is likely to be much better working at the primary level—that is, what are you going to do, rather than at the secondary level, vis-à-vis why are you going to do it.

Many of the legendary stock and commodity traders have referred to the psychological aspects of the markets, and some analysts include market psychology in their analyses. However, this area has always played a minor role and has been relegated simply to one of a number of technical tools. Another case in point is how far afield and misdirected one can be led by conventional wisdom.

For the most direct means of analyzing a market, the hierarchy of tools is represented by the diagram shown in Figure 2-1.

The Mr. Wizard Scenario

Here is a make-believe scenario involving Mr. Wizard, the dean of market advisors serving speculators in the futures

Method of Market Analysis

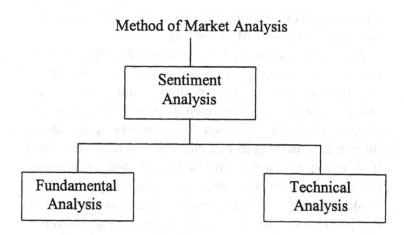

Figure 2-1. Method of market analysis.

markets. This little story may further help to implant in your mind how the market really works.

Mr. Wizard, a market analyst and confirmed numerologist, through a fortunate series of profitable market recommendations in ABC futures, began to develop a significant number of followers. One of his clients, a Mr. Follower, had been making money hand-over-fist and obviously was very high on Mr. Wizard. Mr. Follower had a good friend, Mr. Thomas, whom he frequently urged to subscribe to Mr. Wizard's service and follow his recommendations.

Mr. Thomas had been considering buying ABC when he bumped into his friend, Mr. Follower, who advised him to wait until the 13th of the month, the buy date Mr. Wizard had recommended to his clients. Mr. Thomas, being conservative by nature and from the doubting side of the family, didn't place much faith in numerology. Even so, he decided not to buy now but to wait until the 13th, the buy date Mr. Wizard had recommended—and it wasn't that far off anyway. Furthermore, he'd take only a few long positions in case Mr. Wizard was wrong.

As the 13th approached, the price of ABC began to drop, making Mr. Thomas glad he had waited. The 13th came, Mr. Thomas took his long positions, and sure enough, prices rallied strongly. Well, it could have been a fluke, Mr. Thomas reasoned, but then again, maybe, just maybe, there was something in Mr. Wizard's system. He'd contact his friend and get him to give him Mr. Wizard's recommendation on when to liquidate his positions and go short.

Mr. Follower called Mr. Thomas a week later and said he had just checked Mr. Wizard's phone recording which recommended the 29th as the date to liquidate the position he'd taken on the 13th and to go short. Mr. Thomas still doubted Mr. Wizard's ability, but his previous recommendation had been right and making money, so how could he argue with profits? As the 29th approached, Mr. Thomas kept a watchful eye on prices as they began to move up significantly. Apparently there were relatively few sellers in the market. Finally, the morning of the 29th arrived. Prices opened down somewhat and then began to fall off sharply. "By gosh," Mr. Thomas murmured under his breath, "there must be something in Mr. Wizard's system." He made up his mind right then and there he'd subscribe to the service and continue to follow his recommendations.

Here are the conclusions that can be deciphered from the preceding little scenario:

1. Mr. Thomas postponed his buying before the 13th of the month to see if Mr. Wizard's prediction would materialize. His absence, others like him, and confirmed followers of Mr. Wizard's recommendations reduced the number of would-be buyers in the mar-

ket. Because there was a shortage of buyers, sellers had to reduce their prices in order to attract new buyers.

2. On the 13th, the confirmed followers of Mr. Wizard had buy orders in on the opening; consequently, prices rose. As prices rallied, other followers of Mr. Wizard who were willing to buy on strength and wanted to have an indication that Mr. Wizard's call was on the money, jumped into the market, and the rally was off and running. Furthermore, the rally was fueled by locals on the floor of the exchange who were short and had to cover their positions.

3. On the 29th, the reverse of the foregoing occurred. The absence of sellers in the market immediately prior to the 29th resulted in prices rallying sharply. A heavy preponderance of sellers entering on the 29th, of course, drove prices down rapidly.

In short, these three key points can be drawn from the Mr. Wizard scenario:

1. Mr. Wizard's success was an exercise in self-fulfillment.

2. Mr. Wizard's system, whatever it might have been, was incorrectly given credit for his success. It was a case of doing the right thing for the wrong reason, which has led to the demise of many market analysts and big traders.

3. The secret indicator, which accurately forecasts market prices and which people dream of having for their exclusive personal use, is so obvious that it is obscure. Contrarily, the secret indicator is not secret

at all. Rather, it is the indicator that is best known and most widely used by the majority of participants who are currently trading in the market.

A Real-World Example

In the 1980s, Joe Granville, a widely known and followed stock market analyst, produced a real-life Mr. Wizard scenario. Granville's sell recommendation on January 6, 1981, produced a sell-off and lower market prices that were clearly attributable to his advice alone. Stockholders, believing that his advice was correct, sold their stocks. Although insufficient follow-through failed to develop, this case clearly confirms that "the facts are unimportant—it is what they are perceived to be that determines the course of events." Follow-through would have occurred if a sufficient number of other advisors had turned bearish within the same time frame and had advocated selling. The sell-off then would have been sufficient to begin turning widely followed market indicators bearish, at which juncture the market would have begun to feed off its own negativism. The idea that "buying begets buying and selling begets selling" is very appropriate in the real world. All in all, this is a reflection of the herd instinct which is buried to a greater or lesser degree in each of us.

Why People Trade Futures

If you're wondering why anyone sound of mind would consider getting involved in futures in which a reported 75 to 90 percent of all participants lose, here are some of the principal reasons:

1. The fact that most people lose indicates that the few who win are big winners. It is one of the few, if not the only, legitimate means available where one can start with a few thousand dollars and run it up to a million in a year.
2. The action associated with being involved in the markets is stimulating and exciting. It is Las Vegas every day, and the stakes are even bigger. It's the biggest game anywhere.
3. It is an ego trip to beat the market.

Summary

In entering these markets, you should recognize that you're competing against full-time professionals with many years of experience, and that both the structure of the game and the rules of the exchanges provide significant advantages to the exchange members.

Beating the markets consistently and over the long haul is no easy task, even for the professionals who make it their business. To beat the futures market, hang on to someone else's coattails until you develop confidence and your own style of trading. Even with the foregoing information under your belt and all you can glean from studying the markets, you will be well advised to heed the words, "There is no easy way!"

Chapter 3

MARKET PARAMETERS

One fact is worth a barrel full of speculations

— R. Earl Hadady

Contrary to popular thinking, there are five, not three, basic market parameters. They are:

Price

Volume

Open interest

Market sentiment

Market composition

The present pit system of trading permits only price to be available in real time. Shortly after the market opens on a given day, volume and open interest are available for the prior trading day. Market sentiment data are available daily for the prior trading day. Market composition data as of the close on each of two successive Tuesdays are released every other week, usually on a Friday.

SWISS FRANC (IMM)
Friday, April 17, 1998

	Open	High	Low	Settle	Chg.	Op.Int.
Jun98	.6733	.6756	.6689	.6716	+.0018	61974
Sep98	.6796	.6810	.6777	.6783	+.0019	1274

PV: 11,522   PI: 63265   +977

Figure 3-1. Typcial daily report on trading activity.

Figure 3-1 illustrates a typical daily report of trading activity in the Swiss Franc found in the financial section of a newspaper. Although most of the information is clear, data relating to the opening and the close may not be. There also may be some confusion about the volume and open interest information. These parameters are clarified in later sections of this chapter.

Price

For the new trader, some confusion occasionally arises over both the opening and closing prices.

The **open** is the first price at which a particular futures contract traded at during a specific session.

The **opening range** or **split opening** is the range of prices at which transactions took place immediately after the opening. This situation sometimes occurs when the market is very active, and essentially simultaneous trades occur in different parts of the pit at different prices. These prices are not normally shown in the newspapers.

The **opening bid and ask** prices are reported when no transactions occur immediately after the opening. These prices are not normally shown in the newspapers.

The **high** is the highest price at which a particular futures contract traded at during a specific session.

The **low** is the lowest price at which a particular futures contract traded at during a specific session.

The **close** is the last price at which a particular futures contract traded at during a specific session. However, it is not the official closing price reported by the exchange, and it may not be shown in newspapers. (See settlement price, which follows.)

The **settle or settlement** price is either the **close** or a price representing the range of prices that occurred on the close. The settlement price is used as the official price in determining net gains or losses at the close of each trading session. This is the price you will typically find in the newspapers.

The **change** (Chg in Figure 3-1) is the change in the settlement price from the prior day.

Volume

Volume is the number of contracts traded during a given trading session. In the example of a daily report of trading activity in the Swiss Franc shown in Figure 3-1, volume is listed below the prices as "PV" for the previous trading day's volume. It is the volume for all contracts traded. Note that the volume reported in the newspapers is one day behind prices. The exchanges normally release these data shortly after the next day's trading begins.

A volume of one represents the sale of one contract and the purchase of one contract. Depending on your source of information, volume may be given as a total for all contract months and may not be broken down by contract months. That is the case in Figure 3-1. For detailed analysis, it is sometimes desirable to know the volume by contract month. For example, the volume in one contract month may be expanding while another is declining. This information can help a trader determine which contract month is most appropriate and, in a broad time frame, when best to enter and exit.

Open Interest

Open interest is the total number of open futures contracts in existence at some point in time. An open interest of one consists of one long contract (a purchase) and one short contract (a sale) that offset each other. When reported in the newspapers, open interest, like volume, is one day behind the prices. It is the number of contracts in existence on the close of that day.

Note that the open interest typically reported in the newspapers is the total for all contract months, whereas prices may only cover the most active months. In Figure 3-1, open interest is listed below the prices as "PI" for previous open interest. The sum of the open interest for the two contracts listed is 61,974 + 1,274, which equals 63,248. However, PI is listed as 63,265, which indicates that there is an open interest of 17 in the more distant and not listed December 1998 contract.

Market Sentiment

Market sentiment is the percentage of market participants that are bullish or bearish. For example, a Bullish Consensus of 70 percent for gold would indicate that 70 percent of all of the participants who have positions in the market, regardless of the number of contracts held, believe prices will rise. Conversely, 30 percent are either neutral or believe prices will decline. Although market sentiment cannot be measured as accurately as the other parameters, it is no less a basic market parameter and a vital element in successful trading.

This parameter is discussed in detail in later chapters.

Market Composition

The composition of a specific market can be defined as the type of traders and the extent of their holdings at a given point in time. These data as of the close on two successive Tuesdays are released in a Commitment of Traders Report (COT) issued every other week by the Commodity Futures Trading Commission (CFTC), usually on a Friday.

Contrary Opinion

The COT report was initiated many years ago to minimize the possibility of market manipulation. The CFTC
requires traders holding more than a specified number of
contracts to report their holdings each day. Holding the
minimum number or more contracts is referred to as a
"reportable position." Traders holding reportable positions are classified as hedgers (or commercials), spreaders, and large speculators. Traders holding nonreportable
positions are referred to as small speculators.

Reportable holdings involve a very large number of contracts and need not be of concern to the typical trader, who
falls into the small speculator classification.

A COT Report provides the following information:

1. Percentage of a specific market held by hedgers (commercials), spreaders, large speculators, and small
   speculators.
2. Actual number of traders in each category, other than
   the small speculators.

This parameter and its significance are dealt with in
detail in a subsequent chapter.

Chapter 4

USING SENTIMENT TO ANALYZE THE MARKETS

Wisdom is knowing what to do. Knowledge is knowing how to do it. Success is doing it.

— Author unknown

Market sentiment is a widely known market indicator, yet relatively few think of it or recognize it as a separate and distinct method of market analysis. Traders who are familiar with market sentiment generally refer to it as a technical indicator or tool. It seems ironic that in the more than 100-year history of the stock and futures markets, few, if any, recognized sentiment analysis for what it is—a separate and distinct method of analyzing markets.

What is Sentiment?

Sentiment is a measure of the traders' degree of bullishness or bearishness toward a given futures market. It can

39

be expressed as the percentage of market participants who are either bullish or bearish. For example, at some point in the corn futures market, the Bullish Consensus could be measured and found to be 70 percent. This would mean that 70 percent of all the active participants in this futures market are bullish and expecting higher prices. Stated another way, 7 out of every 10 traders in this market are bullish. The remaining 30 percent, 3 out of 10, are either neutral or bearish and are expecting prices to decline.

Sentiment analysis directly evaluates the source that powers the market, the participants. Why the participants are bullish or bearish is of no consequence.

Limitations of Fundamental and Technical Analysis

For a trader to be successful using fundamental and/or technical analysis, the following sequential events must occur:

1. An analysis must foreshadow a correct market forecast.
2. A position must be taken in the market before the forecast develops; otherwise the position is taken too late.
3. A large unfavorable price move *must not* occur before the forecast develops; otherwise the position is likely to be abandoned with a loss.
4. After a position is taken, the majority of market participants must take similar positions, for whatever reasons, in order to power the market in the forecasted direction.

For a trader using sentiment analysis to be successful, the first three events are not required.

What Moves the Market

Traders are quick to agree that price moves are the result of their own actions, but they often lose sight of this basic and very important fact. Typically, traders seem to become so thoroughly immersed in the myriad fundamental or technical factors that they lose sight of what powers the market. Economics, exports, lines on charts, technical oscillators, and so on *do not* move prices; the actions of market participants power the market and determine prices. The action of the participants is the *only* reason that prices move. Participants buy and sell based on where they think prices are headed—which may or may not be in accord with the underlying facts in the real world. However, if enough market participants believe the market is going to move higher and begin to position themselves accordingly, the market will move higher, regardless of the real-world facts, and conversely.

The accuracy of sentiment analysis to forecast and confirm the trend of a market can be seen in charts of prices versus the Bullish Consensus in Chapter 10.

When a market is highly volatile, the Bullish Consensus may not provide a significant lead-time. However, it provides confirmation of the actual market trend and assurance that taking positions corresponding with this trend are warranted, which is just as important. In other words, you can be reasonably certain that you are on the right

41

side of the market when you trade with the trend of the Bullish Consensus.

When the Bullish Consensus rises through midrange, that is 50, and moves into the 60s, it is a very strong indication that you are not in a bear market. Typically, in a bear market the range of the numbers is below midrange, and in a bull market, above midrange. In a normal market, the Bullish Consensus numbers swing above and below midrange. A number of examples of prices versus the Bullish Consensus are charted in Chapter 10.

The lead-time provided by sentiment numbers is dependent on how fast sentiment is changing. Since there is always some delay in producing sentiment numbers, the lead-time provided by the Bullish Consensus tends to decrease as the volatility of sentiment increases. A volatile sentiment condition in turn produces erratic prices.

A Contrary Opinion Situation

A Contrary Opinion situation is said to exist when most of the traders are of one mind, either bearish or bullish. For example, a Bullish Consensus for gold of 83 percent would indicate such a situation. The consensus states that 83 out of 100 traders in the gold market are bullish and anticipating higher prices ahead. Such a situation offers the potential for making extremely large profits. So many traders are bullish, or in a reverse case bearish, that there are not enough traders left to drive prices any further. Consequently, a very sharp reversal in prices is imminent. In a contrarian situation, indicated by an unusually high or low

Bullish Consensus, a position is taken that is opposite to that of the crowd. For the Bullish Consensus situation of 83% in gold, a short position would be initiated—a position contrary to the prevailing widely held opinion.

A Contrary Opinion situation is sometimes referred to as a heavily oversold or overbought condition. Bullish Consensus numbers above 80 percent or below 20 percent typically signify a Contrary Opinion situation. Historical numbers for past Contrary Opinion situations are the best guide for a particular market. Subsequent chapters provide more details as well as charts of sentiment, the Bullish Consensus versus prices.

Summary

The principle of sentiment analysis is self-evident. If the consensus of the participants in a given market has a significant trend, you know which way prices are going to move. The consensus of the majority becomes a self-fulfilling prophecy.

The bottom line is how well does sentiment analysis work in practice? Forecasting the direction of prices via sentiment analysis is limited only by the ability to precisely measure the degree of sentiment and do it in a timely fashion. A subsequent chapter describes in detail how sentiment, the Bullish Consensus, is produced.

As a corollary to sentiment analysis of markets, consider a preelection poll of voters. Current election polls are typically accurate to within a few tenths of a percent and are generally accepted as gospel. Equivalent accuracy in the polls of the various financial markets is never going to be achieved, but constant and significant improvements are being made.

Using sentiment as a means of market analysis is a system within itself. The reason participants in a particular market are bullish or bearish is irrelevant. Fundamental and technical analyses are *not* involved. One can only conclude that there are three separate and distinct approaches to analyzing the various markets:

1. Sentiment analysis
2. Fundamental analysis
3. Technical analysis

Chapter 5

CONTRARY OPINION

Anyone taken as an individual, is tolerably sensible and reasonable—as a member of a crowd, he at once becomes a blockhead.

— Schiller's dictum

The seemingly illogical price movements that so frequently occur in the futures market are a mystery to the vast majority of traders. Contrary Opinion is involved in all such moves. Although the facts used to explain the workings of Contrary Opinion are widely known, the underlying meaning has escaped most people. It is important to keep in mind that a great deal of difference exists between knowing something and fully recognizing its significance.

Before digging into the workings of Contrary Opinion, a review of the basics of futures markets is in order. Participants in futures effectively buy and sell contracts. For example, a Wheat Contract on the Chicago Board of Trade covers 5,000 bushels of a specified type and grade of wheat. For each transaction there must be a buyer and a seller—the buyer agreeing to accept from the seller the delivery of 5,000 bushels of the specified wheat at a given delivery location during a certain time period at an agreed upon price. In a conventional business transaction of this type, only one contract would normally be drawn between the two parties, the buyer and the seller. However, in the futures market, a clearinghouse is used to guarantee the contracts and as such represents a third party to the transaction. Consequently, two contracts are involved for each transaction—a so-called long contract between the buyer and the clearinghouse and a short contract between the seller and the clearinghouse. However, the clearinghouse is simply a go-between, and the number of long contracts is always exactly equal to the number of short contracts at all times. Thus, there is always a losing contract for every winning contract. Most contracts are not held until the delivery period but rather are liquidated prior to that date.

Trading Attributes

To understand what causes seemingly illogical price moves in the futures markets, a review of the key structural aspects of these markets covered in prior chapters follows:

1. A buyer and seller are required for each transaction.
2. For every winning contract, there is a corresponding losing contract. Note that the reference here is to contracts and *not* participants. There will *not* be a winning participant for every losing participant. Restated, commodity futures trading is a zero-sum game—the dollars won exactly offset the dollars lost.

46

3. At any given moment, the number of either long or short contracts is referred to as the Open Interest. An Open Interest of 10,000 means 10,000 long contracts and 10,000 short contracts exist at the time specified.

Now for the point of the preceding paragraphs. How can 80 percent of market participants be bullish when there is a losing contract for every winning contract? There is only one way. The average bull (bullish participant in the market) must hold only a relatively small number of contracts, whereas the average bear must hold a relatively large number. The reverse would have been true had only 20 percent of the market participants been bullish.

Furthermore, the minority in the market, the 20 percent who are bearish in this instance, must be relatively well financed because they hold a large number of contracts. On the other hand, their opposition is lightly financed and is referred to in the jargon of the pit as "weak hands." Consequently, their actions are much more influenced by the day-to-day price action. A few adverse days will force the "weak hands" to liquidate their positions and retreat to the sidelines. Grasping this idea is vital in understanding how the markets work.

Analyzing Bulls versus Bears

In Chapter 1, the section "Analyzing Winners versus Losers" applies equally to bulls versus bears, which is analyzed in this chapter. Because of its importance, the simple mathematics warrants repeating.

Contrary Opinion

1. Let T stand for all of the traders in the market.

2. Assume a Bullish Consensus of 90 percent, that is, 9 out of 10 traders are bullish and expecting prices to rise. Since T is the total number of traders in the market, then

    90% T = number of traders who are bullish, and

    10% T = number of traders who are bearish

3. Let:

    N_{Bull} = average number of contracts held by a bull, a speculator who is long

    N_{Bear} = average number of contracts held by a bear, a speculator who is short

4. Since the total number of long contracts must equal the total number of short contracts, then

    $$90\% \ T \times N_{\text{Bull}} = 10\% \ T \times N_{\text{Bear}}$$

Thus in this case:

$$N_{\text{Bull}} = \frac{10\% \ T \times N_{\text{Bear}}}{90\% \ T} = \frac{1}{9} N_{\text{Bear}}$$

In other words, on an average, the trader who is long (a bull) holds only one-ninth as many contracts as the trader who is short (a bear).

Based on the above simple analysis, the following tabulation shows the ratio of the average number of contracts held by a Bull versus a Bear for various Bullish Consensus figures:

Contrary Opinion

Bullish Consensus	Ratio of Average Number of Contracts Held by Bull to Bear
5%	19 to 1
10%	9 to 1
15%	5.6 to 1
20%	4 to 1
50%	1 to 1
80%	1 to 4
85%	1 to 5.6
90%	1 to 9
95%	1 to 19

Note that the ratio of bulls to bears changes very rapidly as the extremes are approached. Here is the significance. The reaction in a "contrarian" situation increases drastically for small changes in the Bullish Consensus at extremes. For example, if 90 percent of the speculators in gold believe prices will continue to rise due to inflation, or whatever cause, the drop when it occurs is likely to be quite sharp. However, if the Bullish Consensus is 95 percent rather than 90 percent, the drop is likely to be catastrophic.

A Market Scenario

Using a hypothetical scenario, we can further clarify the workings of the market.

Assume that the entire wheat futures market consists of exactly 100 traders. At the start of the hypothetical trading session that follows, no one has any positions. The bell rings and the session begins:

Yesterday's USDA Crop Production Report was mildly bullish inasmuch as this year's wheat surplus is now estimated to be slightly smaller than originally anticipated. Based on this report, one small trader decides he'd like to buy one contract. Mr. Moneybags, an old and shrewd trader, decides he will accommodate the little bull and sell him one, at the right price, that is—so prices move up a notch.

At this juncture only two people have positions; one is long, the other is short. The Bullish Consensus is therefore 50 percent. Upon seeing the price rise, four little bulls on the sidelines who have been contemplating the purchase of wheat decide they'll take the plunge. They step forward, and each makes a bid for one contract. Mr. Moneybags, being a kindly soul, believes that their wants should be satisfied, but unfortunately the price is too low. He therefore makes an offer at what he believes to be a fair price. After some hesitation, one little bull decides to buy and signals his acceptance. Now three people have positions—two little bulls who are long one contract each and Mr. Moneybags who is short two contracts. The Bullish Consensus is now two bulls to one bear, or 67 percent. The three remaining empty-handed little bulls look nervously at each other, their expressions clearly revealing their displeasure at being left out. Prices are up, and they still don't have contracts. To hell with caution—they start bidding! Up go the prices! Mr. Gotrocks, an astute trader and an old friend of Mr. Moneybags has been patiently watching the action from the sidelines. Upon seeing the prices move up to a level he likes, he signals acceptance of all three bids. Now there are five little bulls in the market, long one contract each, and Messrs. Moneybags and Gotrocks who are short two and three contracts, respectively. The Bullish Consensus at this point is five bulls out of seven participants, or 71 percent.

The trades have hardly been consummated when a wire report states that wheat shipments from Australia have suddenly been curtailed because of a parasite infestation. Five uncommitted little bulls who were still on the sidelines and watching the news now decide to buy. Messrs. Moneybags and Gotrocks agree to accommodate them, again at the right price—the right price being determined by them. The session has just gotten underway, and already the price is up significantly. The ten little bulls who have bought are all smiles and are the envy of the other little bulls who wished they had bought but are still on the sidelines.

At this juncture we have 12 market participants—an Open Interest (number of long or short contracts outstanding) of 12. Messrs. Moneybags and Gotrocks are short (sellers), whereas the 10 little bulls are long (buyers). Summarizing, 10 out of 12 (83 percent) of the traders participating in the market are bullish. In other words, the Bullish Consensus now stands at 83 percent.

News flash! The wire service reports that the U.S. government has just signed a five-year pact with China covering the sale of "umpteen" bushels of wheat each year. The remaining 85 little bulls who are still on the sidelines and have seen the success of their friends are now determined not to be left out. The stampede is on. Messrs. Moneybags, Gotrocks, and three of their friends, Gotsometoo, Highfinance, and Richtoo, want to be helpful, so they quickly offer to sell, again at reasonable prices—the reasonable being at their sole discretion—so prices climb like a shuttle launch from Cape Kennedy. But nevertheless, the 95 little bulls are all smiles. Paper profits have been increasing spectacularly and euphoria abounds. We now have a total of 100 participants in the market—5 big bears and 95 little bulls. The Bullish Consensus now stands at 95 percent. However, the little bulls are too busy counting their paper profits to worry about things like the Bullish Consensus.

News flash! A devastating freak hailstorm has struck central Kansas, laying waste thousands of acres of wheat ready for combining. The little bulls, now with a greedy gleam in their eyes, watch the ticker expectantly. But nothing seems to be happening! The offering (selling) price submitted by several of the big bears has risen, but there are no buyers—there hasn't been a bid for some time. (If you will recall, at the start of our little melodrama, it was assumed for use of illustration that the entire wheat future market consisted of exactly 100 traders—all of whom have positions at this point in our story. Consequently, there are no buyers left who would normally be bidding in order to acquire a position. The little bulls are disappointed, and some think the news just hasn't gotten around yet.

At this point, one little bull, Mr. Firstout, decides that he should take his profits and sell his contract to pay some of his bills. He's anxious because his bills are in arrears, so he offers his contract for sale slightly below the last offering price, which is now void due to the time lapse. Time passes, but there are no takers. Being the nervous type and now more anxious than ever to get out, he solicits a bid from the big bears. Being a kind fellow with a "heart of gold," Mr. Highfinance agrees to help, but unfortunately the price must be much, much lower. As a matter of fact, it must be the lowest price allowed for that day by the exchange— referred to as limit down. Crestfallen but now extremely anxious to get out before all of his profit is gone, Mr. Firstout accepts the bid. The transaction price is posted. The little bulls who were so happy a moment ago stare at the price in disbelief. The news was very bullish, but prices are

down, way down! It must be a mistake! You know, even
the exchanges make an error now and then. A check by
the little bulls reveals that, alas, it is no mistake. The little
bulls now stumble over each other to sell their contracts
and get out of the market. Paper profits have faded, and
some of the little bulls even have losses and must get out.
The only complacent expressions are those worn by the big
bears. Mr. Firstout considers himself lucky, because the
offer he received to buy his contract was the only one
made that day. Prices are locked limit down with no trading going on. The other little bulls are in a panic, but they
must wait for tomorrow.

After a dreadful night's sleep, the little bulls anxiously
await the market opening. The opening bell sounds. The
end of the world has just occurred—the market opens limit
down, and still the big bears are not making any bids.

The end of this little tale is now obvious. The market
continues to drop precipitously until the big bears have
converted all of their paper losses into realized profits.

How the Game Is Played

Now it is time to get the gray matter behind one's eyes in
gear and decipher the significance of this brief scenario.
This little story has revealed how the game is really played.
It is simply a question of identifying the rules as such and
spelling them out so that they are in sharp focus.

Relatively few speculators who participate in the futures
markets have a clear picture of how it really operates—and
this includes some floor traders. To have this insight is

obviously a fantastic advantage, for as the saying goes, "You can't consistently win in any game, unless you know how the game is played!"

Here's what the story revealed in the same sequence as the events unfolded. Highlights are given first, followed by explanatory details:

1. Strong hands (commercials and well-financed traders) took positions opposite (contrary) to what would seem logical based on events (fundamentals). In the real world, the bears are typically represented by the members of the exchange, which consist of the locals who trade for their own account and the commercials (hedgers).

2. Strong hands consistently traded contrary to the news.

3. Strong hands had their edge on every transaction; that is, the trade was consummated at their price.

4. Rising prices and an increasing Bullish Consensus were synonymous, that is, alike in significance.

5. The Bullish Consensus was subject to revision as long as new participants were entering the market, that is, as long as the open interest was changing.

6. Profits could have been made going with the trend of the Bullish Consensus until the consensus reached an extreme.

7. When the market ran out of buyers, prices no longer moved up, regardless of the occurrence of a bullish news event.

8. When the market ran out of buyers, prices could only go one way, down.

9. A news event was not required to produce a precipitous decline. Profit taking by only a handful of speculators is sufficient to start the rock slide.
10. The initial market break resulted from the exit of small traders, not large traders.
11. The break was precipitous once it began.

Here is what can be deduced from the story and the above highlights—and perhaps the most important insights you will ever have into the working of the futures markets:

1. A futures market is basically a money game—not a supply–demand game involving the commodity as commonly presented in literature.

   The typical reaction to the foregoing is, "Futures prices can't get too far out of line with the cash price; otherwise astute traders would jump in and take positions that would bring the market back into line." As the saying goes, "If you believe that, I'll tell you another one." How do you explain moves in soybeans from $12.50 per bushel to $6.50 per bushel in five weeks, or vice versa? No way.

   Keep in mind that the day-to-day cash price is not necessarily indicative of a real-world price, that is, the price that is representative of the balance between actual supply and demand. The immensity of real-world stores and consumption preclude rapid changes in this balance, whereas speculation in the day-to-day cash price market frequently results in price changes of several percent in one day. More on this later.

2. Really big money interests, typically tens of millions of dollars, are involved in major market moves. Once a move gets underway, it is virtually impossible to stop it during the first part of its move. Even though astute traders and hedgers may recognize that prices are out of line with the real world, they simply jump on the bandwagon and go along for the ride. This, of course, adds impetus to the move. They recognize that you simply cannot stem the tide. Here's why. When you are winning, you have leverage and can control roughly $10 with $1. Hence, financially it is easy to continue buying or selling, as the case may be, because $1 buys or sells $10 worth of the futures. On the other hand, when you are losing, you lose your leverage and effectively must have $1 on the line for every $1 you've lost plus margin. Thus, it is relatively easy for big money interests to steamroll over traders with lesser backing. The tide simply rolls on until significant profit taking begins to halt its progress.

3. Price moves may not and often do not have any relation to the real-world fundamentals.

4. The side (bull or bear) with the most money always wins.

This concept of the futures markets fits the facts and explains heretofore unexplainable and illogical price moves—moves that almost invariably have been brushed off by various hogwash terms.

To achieve greater profits, a futures speculator needs to keep in mind at all times the model of the market described in the preceding paragraphs.

Time Frames

So far, we haven't talked about any particular time frame for a market. One time frame is pretty much cut and dried, that is, a single market day. Many floor traders never carry a position overnight, and hence each day is a new beginning for them. A look at a five-minute bar chart of intraday prices looks similar to a daily, weekly, or monthly bar chart, and were it not for the scales, it is not distinguishable from the other charts. In other words, the price action intraday has all of the same characteristics of long time periods. The only differences are that the price swings are smaller and they are accomplished in a shorter span of time.

Intraday, the consensus swings back and forth, and Contrary Opinion situations develop. Such a situation is occurring when the market is described as "stalling out." In this instance, prices were rising as a result of buy orders, which as of now have been executed. Trading activity has dropped to almost nothing. In short, the Bullish Consensus has reached a very high number inasmuch as all of the bulls have committed themselves and there are not enough uncommitted buyers to push prices any higher. In other words, the market is temporarily overbought, and prices will retreat from this level to a lower level as some traders attempt to take profits. Prices will decline until new buyers appear on the scene and a balance between buyers and sellers is struck, or until prices run to the other end of the spectrum and an oversold condition develops. When the market is oversold, there is an absence of sellers, everyone having already sold who intended to sell.

So much for the short one-day time frame. From here on out, the time frames are not as distinct. However, two other time classifications are appropriate: one week and long term. Long term is anything longer than one week, but typically it tends to average around 13 weeks, although it can expand or contract rather drastically.

Let us turn now to the one-week time frame. This period is exemplified by the short covering rallies that so often occur in the last few minutes before the market closes on Friday. Here we have the floor traders who commonly hold a position, usually short, for several days but do not wish to incur the risk of carrying it over a weekend. Some analysts (the author included) believe that, barring some intraweek event that significantly affects the consensus of traders, the tone for the week in a given market is typically set on Monday. Other than the time span, the market conditions described for the one-day frame apply equally to the one-week time frame.

The market conditions described for the one-day and one-week time frames apply to the long-term frame as well. But in this instance, we are dealing with market opinions that have built up gradually over a period of time, and through the process of repeated thinking and evaluation have become cast in concrete, barring a major turn of events. This is the condition that surrounds a major top or bottom in the market and where a Contrary Opinion position can prove to be extremely profitable. This time frame which extends over weeks offers the greatest opportunity for most traders.

Evidence Supporting It's a Money Game

Before summarizing the big picture, it is worthwhile to pull together other supportive evidence that the futures market is indeed a money game, rather than a tug of war between supply and demand as is widely depicted by conventional market wisdom.

1. The principle of Contrary Opinion reveals that the minority of traders consistently win, that is, those who are the better financed.

2. It is an established fact that most speculators lose—typical estimates range from 75 to 95 percent. This reveals that the average trader who wins holds 3 to 19 times as many positions as the average loser; therefore, he must be well financed.

3. Real-life examples such as the 1976–1977 Cook/Hunt incident show that traders with the most money can win, even when positioned contrary to the fundamentals.

4. Conventional wisdom depicts the market as a battle between supply and demand. If this is the case, public speculators should win about 50 percent of the time—certainly not less than 25 percent. Although not directly supportive, it is indicative that conventional wisdom must be wrong.

5. During market hours on any given day, prices for a specific commodity should be relatively stable because almost all fundamental government-collected data are released after the market closes. What then explains moves of several percentage points during one trading session? Pork bellies have even been known to move from one limit to the other and then close within the range—a price move of approximately 6 percent within a single trading

session lasting only a few hours, during which there were no known changes in the fundamentals.

6. Following a bullish or bearish news announcement, not infrequently a strong price move occurs which is in direct opposition to the news.

Some Examples

A couple of hypothetical examples can further cement the above thinking; futures trading is strictly a money game, and it is indeed the modus operandi in the real world.

Example 1: How well would a dyed-in-the-wool technician fare in trading a market in which everyone else was a fundamentalist? Certainly, at times in a market a technician's buy signal coincides with a fundamentalist's idea that the price is right to buy, but in general, it is undoubtedly a losing battle. Also consider the reverse situation in which a fundamentalist is trying to trade in a market where everyone else is a technician. The traders in most markets are an ever-changing mixture of fundamentalists and technicians. Doesn't this explain why a particular market tool works repeatedly for a short time and then suddenly fails to work at all? The balance in the market has shifted from fundamentalists to technicians, or vice versa.

Example 2: Figure 5-1 illustrates the Black Box Concept. Prices for a given market are zipping out of a hole in a black box. Fundamentalists and technicians are standing by examining every parameter of these prices, trying to make heads or tails out of them and taking positions based on their own analysis. However, one astute analyst, after los-

Black Box

Figure 5-1. Black box concept.
The images used herein were obtained from IMSI'S MasterClips
and MasterPhotos Premium Image Collection, 1895 Francisco
Boulevard, East San Rafael, CA 94901.

ing his shirt, decides there must be a better way: Why not look in the box and see what is producing the variations in price? He approaches the rear of the box and looks in. Much to his surprise, he finds it empty. Scratching his head, he then approaches the front of the box from which prices are emanating. He is shocked to find that it is a dark mirror and that it is simply reflecting the prices being bid and offered by the participants.

In summary, the secret price-forecasting indicator, which every trader dreams about and only he or she is privy to, is so obvious that it is not obvious. Contrarily, the secret tool is not secret at all. Rather, it is the tool or combination of tools being used by the majority of participants who are currently trading in the market.

The Principles of Contrary Opinion

It is axiomatic that market prices move as a result of the action of the market participants, regardless of what the facts may be.

When practically all participants are bullish on a particular market and have so positioned themselves, then there is no one left to buy and prices can only go one way from this juncture—down! If practically everyone was bearish on a market, the reverse would have been true—prices would have to move higher.

The principle here is self-evident. If practically all of the buyers, or sellers as the case may be, have fully positioned themselves, there is no one of the same opinion left to participate in the market and drive prices farther—regardless of what fundamental or technical analysis indicates.

The question is frequently asked, "But what will precipitate a price move in a direction opposite to what was expected?" In short, among the vast majority of market participants who are of one mind, bullish or bearish, there are many weak hands in the market, that is, those with relatively limited financing. Furthermore, psychologically they tend to be followers rather than leaders—subscribing subconsciously to the herd instinct. Any adverse move in prices, which could be caused by only a few market participants attempting to take profits, or any adverse news event, produces a rush for the exit by these weak hands. A precipitous move in prices occurs in this situation because there are practically no new or old participants who are willing to take over the positions held by the weak hands at current prices.

In brief, the principles of Contrary Opinion can be stated as follows:

1. Having a Contrary Opinion refers to having an opinion opposite to that held by the majority.

2. Taking a Contrary Opinion position is based on polling market participants and is unrelated to other market analysis methods.

3. Assessment of a poll is based on the number of participants in the market and is *not* related to the number of contracts held by the participants.

4. When approximately 70 percent or more participants are of like mind and get fully positioned in a given market, a Contrary Opinion situation exists. Hence, a price move opposite to the direction expected by the majority is imminent.

5. A fully positioned condition by the majority of participants is revealed when a news event, sup-

porting their position, fails to move prices in the expected direction.

6. The precipitousness of the contrary move is a function of the proportion of participants who are of the same mind.

Chapter 6

HOW MARKET SENTIMENT IS COMPILED

When you can measure what you are speaking about and express it in numbers you know something about it, but when you cannot measure it, when you cannot express it in numbers, your knowledge is a meager and unsatisfactory kind. It may be the beginning of knowledge but you have scarcely in your thoughts advanced to a stage of science

— from the *Popular Lectures and Addresses* of
Lord William Thomson Kelvin in 1891–1894.

Typically, a market research organization obtains sentiment or a consensus on a given subject in most fields by using sampling techniques. Obviously, this method is costly. Fortunately, however, experience in the commodity futures market has shown that there is a simpler and easier way to determine what thousands of traders scattered across the country are thinking.

Most commodity futures traders start out losing money and, for that matter, end up losing. As a result of mounting losses, most traders conclude that they must be doing something wrong, abandon their own method of trading, and seek the advice of professional market analysts. Therefore, to quantify market sentiment and produce a Bullish Consensus, it is only necessary to:

1. Ascertain each analyst's recommendations.
2. Weight each analyst's advice based on the number of traders following his or her advice.
3. Weight each analyst's advice based on the specificity of the advice.

Analyst's Recommendations

Clearly, more traders follow the recommendations of analysts in large brokerage firms than those in smaller firms. The number of clients a specific brokerage firm has is estimated by first establishing the number of commodity brokers the firm employs. Based on knowledge that a single broker can only handle so many clients, the average number of clients per broker can then be estimated. Some brokers may only handle 1 or 2 large clients, whereas another broker may handle 30. However, because a large number of brokers are involved, using an average number of clients per broker is a valid approach. Bear in mind that what is important is the number of clients, not the dollar value of the business being transacted. Some large brokerage firms specialize in handling commercial business for a relatively small number of accounts and hence deal in a large number of contracts having a high dollar value. However, such firms have a relatively low weighting factor because they influence relatively few traders. Again, remember that the important factor here is the number of traders that are influenced, not the number of contracts involved.

With regard to independent market analysts who publish advisory letters, the number of traders influenced is simply proportional to the number of their subscribers.

Currently, approximately 100 sources distribute professional trading recommendations on the most widely followed futures. As you might suspect, this list is in a state of constant revision.

The frequency of advice from the various advisors ranges from daily hot lines to monthly newsletters. As it became increasingly important to have timely Bullish Consensus numbers, daily as opposed to weekly polling was initiated in October 1988. A special computer program was developed for inputting the polling data each day and deriving a separate Bullish Consensus for approximately 30 different futures.

Advice Specificity

In addition to weighting advisors based on the number of estimated traders who follow their advice, it is necessary to weight the specificity of their opinions. Recommendations range all the way from an inclination such as "am leaning to the bullish side" to a "buy at the market," and then there are some that are undecipherable. Obviously, a strong, well-supported market opinion will influence more followers to act than a weak one. The weighting which the Bullish Consensus applies to opinions uses a scale of nine numbers, that is, 0 to 8 with 0 being the bearish extreme, 4 neutral, and 8 the bullish extreme. This provides four gradations each side of neutral, which is about as close as one can judge the intent of someone's market comments and recommendations.

The consensus in some markets, such as foreign currencies, interest rates, and the stock market, can change overnight as a result of government intervention – for example, when the government buys or sells dollars in the cash market to support or depress a foreign currency. The foregoing should be considered when using the Bullish Consensus to trade in these markets.

Bullish Consensus Scale

To facilitate its use, the Bullish Consensus is scaled from 0 to 100 percent. The extreme of 0 percent means that everyone is unequivocally bearish and expecting prices to move lower, 50 percent is neutral, and 100 percent means everyone is unequivocally bullish and is expecting prices to move higher. Typically, the Bullish Consensus numbers tend to stay in the range of 30 to 70 percent. At 30 percent an oversold condition is beginning to develop, whereas at 70 percent an overbought condition is developing. Oversold refers to a market condition in which there is a scarcity of buyers, whereas overbought refers to a scarcity of sellers. As the extremes of 0 percent and 100 percent are

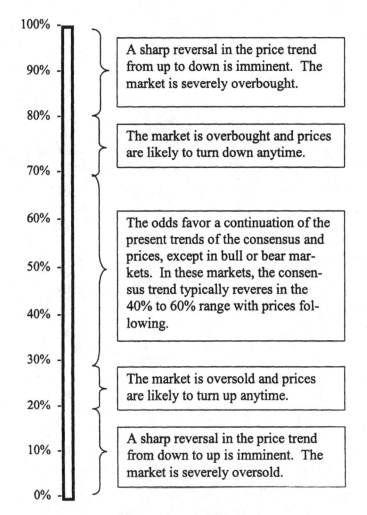

Figure 6-1. Bullish consensus meter.

approached, a reversal in the trend of the consensus and prices becomes more and more probable and imminent. The Bullish Consensus Meter in Figure 6-1 depicts the significance of the percentage figures.

Chapter 7

HISTORY OF MARKET SENTIMENT

When everyone thinks alike, everyone is likely to be wrong.

— Humphrey B. Neill

Contrary Opinion, as applied to the futures markets, is by definition an opinion opposite to the view held by the majority of the market participants. If the majority are bullish and expecting prices to rise, a contrarian—one who holds a Contrary Opinion—will be bearish and expecting prices to decline. The reverse will also be true.

The following summarizes the history of Contrary Opinion.

Charles Mackay, LL.D, 1814–1889: The First to Document Contrarian Events

In 1841, some 150 years ago, Charles Mackay wrote a delightful book, *Memoirs of Extraordinary Popular Delusions*.

During the course of being reprinted and republished several times, the title was changed to *Extraordinary Popular Delusions and Madness of Crowds*.[1] The book deals with three financial delusions, as well as those involving alchemists, prophecies, fortune telling, the Crusades, witches, and other follies.

Oddly enough, Mackay's vocations were song-writer, poet, and journalist. However, his excursion into authoring a number of books resulted in the above-mentioned classic, which deserves space on everyone's financial book shelf.

Mackay's book will show you that history is strewn with numerous delusions. Two of the more widely known and often quoted financial delusions are "The Mississippi Scheme" and "Tulipomania." They involved what we now refer to as Contrary Opinion situations.

Mississippi Scheme

In France in the early eighteenth century, John Law, the son of a Scottish banker, formed and sold stock in the Mississippi Company, a venture to develop the Louisiana Territory in North America. It was generally believed that an abundance of gold, silver, and precious stones were to be found in the Louisiana Territory. The initial stock offering was at 400 livers in 1716. So frenzied was the buying that by 1720, just four years later, the stock had appreciated 40 times from the original offering. People poured in from the countryside to buy the stock and watch the market as the price catapulted upward day-by-day, creating paper profits that were mind-boggling. Eventually, of course, there were no more buyers to enter the market, and investors began to realize that the fundamental value of the stock could actually be far below its current market price. An uneasiness set in, which eventually turned to panic. In short order the market collapsed, and thousands of individuals were left holding stock that was essentially worthless.

Tulipomania

This financial delusion is also referred to as Tulip Mania. The word "tulip," which is believed to have come from a Turkish word signifying a turban, was introduced into Europe in the mid-1500s. The demand for tulips kept steadily increasing during the decades that followed and were much sought after, especially by the wealthy in Holland and Germany. By 1634, a man of means who was without a collection of tulips was thought to be exhibiting bad taste. The rage for tulips finally spread to the middle class and became so great that preposterous prices were paid. For example, as much as 6000 florins (about 560 pounds sterling) was paid for a single unique bulb. By 1636, regular marts for the sale of tulips were established on the stock exchanges of Amsterdam and other cities. People of all economic levels sold their property and invested in tulips. The prudent, recognizing that this folly could not last forever, began to sell. The trickle of sellers who did not reinvest in tulips soon became a stream. Almost overnight the stream became a river that swept the wealth of the majority into the hands of a few.

In each of these examples, prices rose spectacularly as eager and unthinking buyers were caught up in the temporary madness of the time. In each case, the end result was always the same: When practically everyone had bought, who was left to buy? With the absence of buyers, there was only one direction for prices to go: down. Once prices turned lower, the rush of former buyers to sell in order to realize their paper profits, and/or avoid losses, created a panic, with a resultant crash in prices.

Other Examples

You might be inclined to think that such public follies as the Mississippi Scheme and Tulipomania are rare. Nothing could be further from the truth. Major public delusions of more recent vintage are the "Crash of 29" and the "Crash of 87."

Humphrey B. Neill, 1895–1977: Dean of Contrary Opinion

Although there are numerous recorded instances of Contrary Opinion in action, Humphrey B. Neill was the first to focus on the idea of contrary thinking and to use it in investment analysis. His first work was a pamphlet entitled "It Pays to Be Contrary," published in 1951. This information was later incorporated in the book, *The Art of Contrary Thinking*,[2] first published in 1954 and since reprinted a number of times.

Neill wrote and published a highly respected financial letter, "Neill's Letters of Contrary Opinion," from 1947 until his death in 1977. During this period, he held annual Contrary Opinion Forums at the Equinox House in Manchester, Vermont, until around 1973 and later at the Basin Harbor Club near Vergennes, Vermont. These forums attracted top financial experts from around the country. His letter and work have been continued and extended by James L. Fraser, a highly respected analyst and proponent of the Contrary Opinion investment philosophy.

In view of Humphrey Neill's original work and thinking, he is generally regarded, and rightfully so, as the Dean of Contrary Opinion. His work covered the broad application of Contrary Opinion into many fields, with emphasis on the financial area and, more specifically, the stock market.

In reviewing Neill's work, you will find that he viewed Contrary Opinion in a much more generalized manner than we do today. To give you the benefit of his thinking, which hopefully is not out of context, a number of key paragraphs from his book, *Art of Contrary Thinking,* follow:

> Having concentrated for many years on the study of the theory of Contrary Opinion, I believe it is correct to say that the theory is more valuable in avoiding errors in forecasting than in employing it for definite forecasting. (p.100)

> No problem connected with the Theory of Contrary Opinion is more difficult to solve than: (a) how to know what prevailing general opinions are; and (b) how to measure their prevalence and intensity. (p.156)

> Theory of Contrary Opinion is NOT a system of forecasting, but rather it is a method of working toward thought-out conclusions. (p. 160)

Contrary opinions do not forecast, but they do check others' forecasts! (p. 161)

The chief "catch" in the Contrary Opinion Theory seems to be that readers persist in looking upon it as a forecasting tool or system, whereas, in actuality, it is an antidote to careless and fruitless predictions. (p. 173)

Based on the preceding paragraphs, it is clear that Neill never viewed Contrary Opinion as an indicator to provide buy or sell signals in the financial markets. Consequently, he never attempted to quantify Contrary Opinion.

Abraham W. Cohen, 1910–1983: First to Use Contrary Opinion as an Indicator

Credit for being the first to use Contrary Opinion as a definitive market indicator goes to Abraham W. Cohen. As a result of his studies in the early 1960s, he developed a means for quantifying Contrary Opinion. This marked a major advancement. Cohen, recognizing that polling a representative sampling of stock market speculators and investors in a timely fashion was impractical, directed his attention to polling advisors. His rationale was that a consensus of the market opinions of advisors could probably be equated with a representative sampling of the public. This thinking proved to have merit, thus making it possible to quantify Contrary Opinion for the first time and apply it to the stock market.

Cohen's indicator was based on the percentage of advisory services that were bearish. He rationalized that since most advisors are trend followers, they are most bearish at market bottoms and least bearish at market tops. Thus, he reasoned that his Bearish Sentiment Index would provide a reliable indicator of turning points in the market—that is, Contrary Opinion situations. As well as graphing his Index, Cohen provided a tabular breakdown of the percentage of bears, bull, and neutrals.

The Sentiment Index originated by Cohen was first published in January 1963 as a monthly market letter entitled "Investors Intelligence."[3] In 1964 it was converted to a semimonthly service, and in June 1969 it went weekly. Mr. Cohen died in 1983, but his work is being continued by Michael Burke.

James H. Sibbet, 1914–1995: First to Grasp the Basics of Contrary Opinion

In Pasadena, California, in the early 1960s, James H. Sibbet became interested in Humphrey Neill's work in Contrary Opinion. Sibbet was a well-known stock market analyst and publisher of a market letter, "Cumulative Average," which had a national following numbering in the thousands. He became an ardent student, admirer, and follower, up to a point, of Humphrey Neill. In 1964, using his own ideas, Sibbet began to experiment with the idea of using Contrary Opinion to provide buy and sell signals in what at that time was referred to as the commodity (now futures) markets.

Although Sibbet used market advisors as his source of data, just as Cohen did, his concept for quantifying market

77

sentiment was entirely different. Cohen's indicator was a plot of just the bearish sentiment, whereas Sibbet classified everyone—bulls, bears, neutrals, and no opinions—on a single scale. This was his first major contribution. Sibbet believed it was important to include neutrals and no opinions because they represented a sector of the market. He rationalized that all participants in the market must be considered since, by definition, a true Contrary Opinion situation requires the majority of market participants to be bullish, or vice versa. He referred to his sentiment scale as the Bullish Consensus having a range of 0 to 100 percent.

Sibbet's ideas were right on. The first several signals provided profitable trades. Subsequent erroneous signals led to a review of his concept and a vital change in the procedure he used for deriving the Bullish Consensus. This all-important change was Sibbet's second major contribution. To each advisory service included in his survey he assigned a weight proportional to the estimated number of market participants it influenced. In short, this enabled Sibbet's Bullish Consensus numbers to more closely represent an actual consensus of all the traders in the market. This modification revealed a depth of understanding that was not previously present. It opened the door to a more precise measurement of the consensus and its use as a market indicator.

As the first step in calculating his Bullish Consensus, Sibbet assigned an arbitrary weight to each opinion source. This weight was retained and used each week, barring a change in the source's business. Opinions (O) were rated as 0 for bearish, 50 for neutral, and 100 for bullish.

Sibbet calculated his weighted Bullish Consensus (BC_W) using the following formula:

$$BC_W = \frac{\text{Sum of all weighted opinions}}{\text{Sum of all weighted opinions if they were bullish}}$$

The merit of Sibbet's concept can be easily seen by comparing a weighted and unweighted consensus of five hypothetical firms. Assume that four firms are small and have roughly the same number of followers. The fifth firm, however, is very large and influences 10 times as many clients as any one of the other firms. Now, take the case where the four small firms are bearish, whereas the big firm is bullish.

In the above case of five hypothetical firms, and using 0 to designate bearish and 100 bullish, the unweighted Bullish Consensus (BC_U) is:

$$BC_U = \frac{(4 \text{ sources} \times 0) + (1 \text{ source} \times 100)}{(5 \text{ sources} \times 100)}$$

$$= \frac{0 + 100}{500} = 0.2 = 20\%$$

When weighted, which recognizes that one source has 10 times as much influence as each of the other four, the Bullish Consensus is:

$$BC_W = \frac{(4 \text{ sources} \times 0 \times 1 \text{ wgt.}) + (1 \text{ source} \times 100 \times 10 \text{ wgt.})}{(4 \text{ sources} \times 100 \times 1) + (1 \text{ source} \times 100 \times 10)}$$

$$= \frac{0 + 1000}{1400} = 0.71 = 71\%$$

79

To express the above numbers as percentages, a multiplier of 100 is required, which makes them 20 percent and 71 percent, respectively.

Weighting, in this example, changes the Bullish Consensus from 20 percent, a bearish condition, to 71 percent a bullish situation—a complete about-face in significance. Actually, the numbers are conservative because the disparity among advisors and brokerage firms is considerably greater than 10 to 1. As a matter of fact, when weighting is *not* used, it provides ambiguous and inconsistent answers.

The preceding makes clear that an unweighted consensus can easily hide changes in opinion that would readily be apparent if weighting were used.

Based on his insights into the workings of Contrary Opinion, Sibbet initiated a weekly advisory letter for the commodity futures market in 1964. He named the letter "Market Vane," since its goal was to point the way to profits through the use of Contrary Opinion. The idea came from a weather vane pointing the direction of the wind. As a result of his work, which quickly became recognized nationwide, Sibbet was invited to lecture at Neill's Contrary Opinion Forum in Vermont in 1967. It is believed that Sibbet coined the word "contrarian" when he used it during his lecture.

R. Earl Hadady, 1920– : Developer of the Theory of Contrary Opinion

In May of 1971, Sibbet and Hadady formed the California corporation, Sibbet-Hadady Publications, Incorporated, to provide both stock and commodity market advisory services. Sibbet was concerned primarily with market analysis, whereas most of Hadady's time was devoted to business matters. The company continued in this vein until June 1974, when an amicable parting between the principals took place. Hadady purchased Sibbet's share of the company, and the firm subsequently became Hadady Corporation. Sibbet turned his full attention to the gold and silver markets and formed the firm, Sibbet Publications, to publish the market letter, "Let's Talk Silver and Gold."

The author's deepening involvement in writing and lecturing on Contrary Opinion revealed the need for a brief and sharply focused picture of the mechanics of how and why Contrary Opinion works. Statements such as "When everyone thinks alike, they are likely to be wrong," and "The majority can never be right at major market turns," always raised the big question, "Why not?" It also raised the question of why the statement "everyone is most bullish at the top, and most bearish at the bottom" is valid. The author's efforts to produce a clearer picture of Contrary Opinion resulted in the analyses covered in Chapters 1 and 5.

Sibbet's early system of applying arbitrary weights to each independent advisor and brokerage firm was based on judgment that made it somewhat inaccurate. The author originated the more precise system as described in Chapter 6.

In the late 1980s, the volatility of trader sentiment began to increase, producing a corresponding volatility in the markets. It became increasingly evident that daily, rather than weekly, Bullish Consensus numbers would be a tremendous asset to traders. Daily compilation of Bullish Consensus data began in October 1988.

Market sentiment was initially thought to be of value only in identifying Contrary Opinion situations. It was subsequently recognized that the trend of the market actually reflects the trend of market sentiment. Thus, when using market sentiment as an indicator, you trade with the trend of market sentiment until it reaches an extreme value, and then you take a contrarian position.

Another facet of market sentiment uncovered in recent years is highly useful in identifying the general market environment, bear, normal, or bull. In a bear market the Bullish Consensus stays below midrange, typically from about 30 to 50 percent. In a normal market the Bullish Consensus ranges from about 35 to 65 percent. For a bull market the sentiment stays above midrange and ranges from about 50 to 70 percent.

Perhaps the author's most significant contribution to the understanding of Contrary Opinion was his recognition of sentiment as a separate and distinct means of analyzing the markets as compared to fundamental or technical analysis. Fundamental and technical analyses are the bases of why traders take specific positions. Sentiment analysis is not concerned with "why," but only with "what" positions are being taken in a market. Thus, neither technical nor fundamental analyses are involved when using market sentiment to take a position.

The author summarizes his contributions to Contrary Opinion as follows.

1. Identifying sentiment analysis as a separate and distinct means of analyzing the markets vis-à-vis fundamental and technical.

2. Replacing the system of assigning arbitrary weights to opinions with a more precise weighting system, thus enabling a more accurate Bullish Consensus.

3. Developing a simple mathematical expression that reveals why these typical statements are true:

   a. "When everyone thinks alike, they are likely to be wrong."

   b. "The majority can never be right at major market turns."

   c. "Everyone is most bullish at the top and most bearish at the bottom."

   d. "The better financed traders usually win."

4. Recognizing that the range of the Bullish Consensus numbers identifies the type of market condition, that is bear, normal, or bull.

5. Producing daily Bullish Consensus numbers.

Notes

1. *Extraordinary Popular Delusions and Madness of Crowds* is available from Fraser Publishing Company, P.O. Box 494, Burlington, Vermont 05402. Phone (800) 253-0900, Fax (802) 658-0260, Web Site/e-mail: fraserbooks.com

2. *The Art of Contrary Thinking* is available from Fraser Publishing Company, Box 494, Burlington, Vermont, 05402. Phone (800) 253-0900, Fax (802) 658-0260, Web Site/e-mail: fraserbooks.com

3. "Investors Intelligence," a market letter, is available from Chartcraft, Incorporated, 30 Church Street, New Rochelle, New York, 10801. Index data is available since its origin in

January 1963. Phone (914) 632-0422, Fax (914) 632-0335, Web Site: chartcraft.com

4. "Bullish Consensus," a market newsletter, is available from Market Vane Corporation, P.O. Box 90490, Pasadena, CA 91109-0490, Phone (626) 395-7436, Fax (626) 795-7654, e-mail: marketvane@ earthlink.net. Originally the Bullish Consensus was a feature of the market letter, *Market Vane*, published by James H. Sibbet, Web Site: marketvane.net

Chapter 8

MARKET COMPOSITION

Not knowing the facts is courting disaster.

— R. Earl Hadady

Market composition pertains to the proportion of the market held by different types of traders on a specific date. The types of traders are classified by the Commodity Futures Trading Commission (CFTC) as hedgers (or commercials), spreaders, large speculators, and small speculators.

Individuals and companies, or their brokers, who hold so-called reportable positions are required to report their holdings daily to the CFTC. This information is the basis of two Commitment of Traders (COT) Reports that are released every other week. However, these reports only cover two specific days during the preceding two-week period, Tuesday and the preceding Tuesday. Reports are typically issued on a Friday or Monday. Thus, for the most recent Tuesday, the data are three to four days old.

Failure to produce and release daily data to all speculators tends to favor the floor traders. Floor transactions tend to reveal the actions taken by the largest players in the market, the hedgers (commercials) and large speculators.

As of October 1, 1993, the Commodity Futures Trading Commission (CFTC) ceased direct distribution of COT Reports. Instead, the CFTC routinely makes COT data available on their web site[1] and through a variety of intermediaries.

Definition of Terms

Terms used in COT Reports relative to market composition are defined as follow:

Hedger (often referred to as a **"commercial"**). Anyone in the business of producing or processing a commodity traded on a futures market who wants to hedge and buys/sells a number of futures contracts equal to or in excess of the minimum reporting level (see definition below). The hedger or the hedger's broker is required to report the hedger's position each day to the CFTC. Here is an example of a hedger whose position must be reported each day. A Kansas farmer, who is expecting to harvest about 800,000 bushels of wheat in early August, sells 800,000 bushels (160 contracts) of wheat in the futures market in early April, four months prior to harvest. The current reporting level for wheat is 100 contracts, 500,000 bushels. Note that after taking his hedging position in the futures market, price fluctuations in wheat are no longer of concern to the farmer. What he may lose in the futures market he will gain in the cash crop and conversely.

86

Spreader. Anyone holding contracts equal to or in excess of the minimum reporting level in two different contract months as long as they are (1) balanced, (2) in the same futures, and (3) in the same market. Balancing is without regard to which crop year/calendar year is involved. Spreaders are required to report or have their broker report their position each day to the CFTC.

Large Speculator. Anyone other than a hedger or spreader holding contracts equal to or in excess of the minimum reporting level in any contract month at any given time. Large speculators are required to report or have their broker report their position each day to the CFTC.

Small Speculator. Anyone who does not fall into any of the above categories. Traders in this category are *not* required at any time to report the number of contracts held to the CFTC.

Open Interest. The total number of outstanding futures contracts in a given contract month for a specific commodity at the close of a given trading session. Since there must be a long contract for every short contract, and vice versa, one long contract and one short contract represent an open interest of one. Open interest does not include open futures contracts against which notices of delivery have been issued by the clearing organization of an exchange.

Reporting Level. The minimum number of futures contracts in anyone's holdings which must be reported each day to the CFTC. The report must specify the number of contracts, the contract months, and whether the holder of those contracts is speculating or hedging. There is no reporting requirement when the number of contracts held is less than the reporting level.

Market Composition Example

For general analysis of the data in a COT Report, it is helpful to assemble the data in the following format:

Wheat Futures on the Chicago Board of Trade
August 29, 1995

Type of Trader	Long		Short	
	Pct.	No.	Pct.	No.
Large hedgers (commercials)	33.7	55	05.9	24
Large spreaders (12 traders)	03.9	12	03.9	12
Large speculators	31.8	31	56.8	51
Small speculators	30.6		33.4	
	100.0 %		100.0 %	

Keep in mind that data from these reports *cannot* be used to determine whether a contrarian trade exists. A contrarian trade requires the majority of traders to be on the same side of the market; such information cannot be gleaned from a COT Report.

Although relatively few traders have large enough positions to be classified as reportable, information in COT Reports is useful:

1. In evaluating the potential of a contrarian trade
2. As a separate trading tool

How to Evaluate the Potential of a Contrarian Trade

Market composition is particularly important in evaluating a contrarian trade because large potential gains can be achieved only if a large number of traders can be forced to liquidate their positions, either voluntarily or involuntarily, at a loss. Remember that the futures market is a zero-sum game. For a contrarian to win, the large majority of traders must lose.

Small traders, who are poorly financed, are the most easily dislodged from their positions in the market, followed by the large speculators. Note that hedgers (commercials) are essentially out of the market since they hold futures positions that are approximately balanced by their actuals. Hence, the ideal contrarian position is opposite to (1) many small traders, and (2) few large speculators and hedgers. Restated, a good contrarian position is likely to be shared by a majority of the hedgers and large speculators and a minimum number of small traders—thus placing a person on the same side of the market as the better financed traders.

Hedgers, by virtue of their position in actuals, have essentially removed themselves from both the cash and futures market, which is the basic purpose and function of a futures market. Consequently, price fluctuations in futures have little, if any, effect on the gain or loss from

89

positions held by a hedger. What hedgers may be losing in the futures market, they will be gaining in the cash market, and conversely. However, hedgers do affect the market. First, even with the best planning, their offsetting positions of cash versus futures are never exactly balanced. Second, rather than making/taking delivery in the futures market, hedgers frequently deliver/receive their cash commodity elsewhere and at the same time offset their positions in the futures market. Third, some hedgers intentionally speculate by not balancing their offsetting positions. In any event, the offsetting activity of hedgers can and often does affect futures market prices because so many contracts are involved.

In most futures, the preponderance of hedging is on the short side by producers—not the long side by processors who can usually pass along any unanticipated cost increases of the commodity to the consumer. Because the majority of the hedgers normally share a good contrarian trade, such a trade is more likely to be on the short side rather than the long side. However, in the COT Report covering wheat provided earlier in this chapter, this is not the case—the hedging is primarily processors who are long. The large traders favor the short side, whereas the small speculators are about equally balanced.

When the long hedgers, the processors, begin to offset their positions, prices tend to be depressed because they will have to sell to liquidate their long positions. Conversely, when short hedgers, the producers, begin to offset their positions, the effect is to boost prices because they have to buy to cover their short positions.

Historical data from the COT Reports can be helpful in determining the time periods during which the hedgers on both sides of the market typically exit.

A Separate Trading Tool

A trend in the posture, long or short, of the major money interests is generally opposite to the posture of the majority of small speculators. Remember: Someone has to be selling if the majority of small speculators are buying, and vice versa. Hence, the trend of the data from successive issues of the COT Reports can be used as a separate trading tool. As has been shown elsewhere in this book, the major money interests in the market consistently win. Thus, it can prove profitable to track them and join them afterward, but only after prices stabilize. This is an indication that the small speculators are fully positioned and that the price trend that has been going against the major money interest is about to change.

Data in COT Reports are several days old, even on the day a report is issued. Furthermore, the data become increasingly old between issues. Because these data are never current, initially it was thought to have little value as a trading tool. This turned out not to be the case, however. Curtis Arnold, while working at Weiss Research,[2] deserves the credit for recognizing the value and developing a method for analyzing the data. At that time, the COT Reports were only issued monthly, and the data were about 11 days old when released. Hence, their value was somewhat restricted. Consequently, Arnold's original work, the WOW Index (an acronym for "Who Owns What"), met with limited success and is no longer published. The COT data, which are released every other week, is three and eight trading days old. Though certainly an improvement, in this age of computers, the CFTC should be able to make the data available daily.

To decipher the activity of the hedgers and large speculators, you will need to plot the trend of data in successive reports and keep in mind their modus operandi as covered in the following paragraphs.

If short hedging is increasing, producers are likely to view current prices as being close to the highest price they are likely to see. Producers want to hedge at the highest possible price to maximize profits, or in some cases, to minimize losses. Sales of a large number of futures contracts will increase the selling pressure, resulting in lower prices.

If long hedging is increasing, processors are likely to view current prices as being close to the lowest price they are likely to see. Processors want to hedge at the lowest possible price to maximize profits or, in some cases, to minimize losses. Purchases of a large number of futures contracts will increase the buying pressure, resulting in higher prices.

If the percentage of large speculators who are short is increasing, they view the market as moving lower in the near future and want to sell more contracts to increase their profits. Conversely, if the percentage is decreasing, they believe they have made a mistake and are exiting, believing prices are going to move higher.

If the percentage of large speculators who are long is increasing, they view the market as moving higher in the near future and want to buy more contracts to increase their profits. Conversely, if the percentage is decreasing, they believe they have made a mistake and are exiting, believing prices are going to move lower.

Notes

1. Commodity Futures Trading Commission, Three Lafayette Center, 1155 21st Street, Washington, DC, 20581. Phone (202) 418-5000 Economics Division, Phone (202) 418-5260, Fax (202) 418-5524 Web Sites: cftc.gov (general information), cftc.gov/dea/cot.html (COT Rept.)
2. Weiss Research, Inc., 4176 Burns Road, Palm Beach Gardens, FL 33410, Phone (800) 291-8545, (561) 627-3300, Fax (561) 625-6685 Web Site: martinweiss.com, E-mail: mdw@weissinc.com

Chapter 9

TRADING TO WIN

The key to success isn't much good until one discovers the right lock to insert it in.

— Tehyi Hsieh, Chinese Epigrams Inside Out
and Proverbs 1948

This next to the last chapter represents the bottom line; how you can use the Bullish Consensus for profitable trading in the futures markets. But if you have been searching for the Holy Grail, you're doomed to disappointment: "There's ain't no such animal." If you're a realistic and practical trader, the Bullish Consensus will significantly improve your batting average. As a reminder, the better traders in the business rarely bat more than 500, but that is enough to win big.

Before discussing how to initiate trades with unusually big profit potentials by using the consensus, let's run the vital principles of the futures markets by one more time, just to be certain they're clearly in mind.

Market Principles

1. The futures markets are money games.
2. The cash markets are money games.

95

3. The real-world price of a commodity predicated on the balance between actual supply and demand
   a. Changes very slowly because of the magnitudes involved.
   b. Serves only as an imaginary price around which future and cash prices gyrate wildly.

4. The game is structured so that the side of the market with the smaller number of traders consistently wins because those traders are better financed.

5. The better financed traders consistently trade contrary to the prevailing news and market opinions. If they didn't, who would be selling when most traders are buying, and conversely?

6. The conventional market wisdom is a prescription to failure. Otherwise, why would so many lose?

7. Trying to decipher the market fundamentals serves no useful purpose. It is a substantial task in itself, yet assuming success, you could still lose.

8. Since the news and most market letters are concerned with the fundamentals, they are typically of little help in making profitable trading decisions.

9. Keeping abreast of the news and fundamentals is desirable only at critical points in the market; otherwise it robs you of time, distracts you, and subconsciously influences your actions.

10. The trend of the Bullish Consensus accurately depicts the trend of prices in a futures market and identifies the side of the market to be on until an extreme is reached.

Using the Bullish Consensus to Trade

There are two ways to use the Bullish Consensus to trade futures:

1. As your basic analytical trading tool
2. In combination with fundamental and/or technical analysis

The sections that follow are devoted to these two approaches to trading.

The Bullish Consensus as Your Basic Analytical Tool

To use the Bullish Consensus as your basic analytical tool, you will need:

1. Daily Bullish Consensus numbers.
2. A recent plot of prices for the past several months versus the Bullish Consensus, which will provide you with a visual picture of the current market, bull, bear, or normal. During a bull market, the Bullish Consensus numbers tend to range between roughly 45 and 75; in a bear market between roughly 25 and 55; in a normal market between roughly 30 and 70.
3. Historical daily Bullish Consensus numbers are vital. Historical data, preferably in the form of a chart of the consensus versus prices, will provide you with a convenient frame of reference. For a particular

97

futures, these data are your best guide to consensus numbers representing tops and bottoms, how long a time high or low numbers are likely to persist before a price break occurs, and so on. Historical data[1] back to 1970 can be acquired for the various futures.

4. A daily bar chart of prices.

5. Daily market news but only when the Bullish Consensus indicates that a major top or bottom seems imminent. Unfortunately, the news on the futures you're planning to trade isn't always forthcoming at the right time. Given an ideal situation you'd like:

a. Bearish news, a low Bullish Consensus (BC), and prices that refuse to decline. This is an indication that the majority of the bears are fully positioned (short) and that a major bottom is at hand. You'll want to buy immediately.

b. Bullish news, a high BC, and prices that refuse to rise. This is an indication that the majority of the bulls are fully positioned (long) and that a major top is at hand. You'll want to sell immediately.

6. Commitment of Traders Report as often as issued by the Commodity Futures Trading Commission. Occasionally, this report is of some help, but the delay in availability limits its usefulness.

The large speculators will typically be trading against the trend of the consensus. Therefore, when it appears that the consensus and price trend are topping out, you will want to immediately join the large speculators, since we know that the traders with the most money consistently win.

Plotting the trend of the net position of large speculators, longs minus shorts, can provide you with a picture of what the "deep pockets" are doing. The large hedgers (commercials) are effectively out of the market since their futures positions are offset by actuals. However, their actions often can and do affect prices as they liquidate what typically are large positions. For details on the Commitment of Traders Report, see Chapter 8.

Using the Bullish Consensus to trade is simplicity itself. In general, the absolute consensus numbers are not as important as the trend of the numbers, a trend reversal, and historically high or low numbers. In broad terms, you trade with the trend of the Bullish Consensus until the trend reverses itself or an extreme is reached, at which point you reverse your position. Two terms in the preceding sentence need to be defined, *trend* and *extreme*.

Trend. Be aware that a tradable trend, in a given futures, is not always present. When such a nontrending condition exists, it is better to stand aside and wait until an appropriate trend develops. This may take days, weeks, or even months. Don't feel you have to trade and be in the market all the time. Being of this mind is a prescription for how to lose. Many of the more successful traders are in the market only a few times each year. They wait for what they believe to be the right opportunity, and then they commit heavily.

A short-term, bullish trend is normally defined as three or more successive days in which the numbers are rising or unchanged for one of the days. Contrariwise, a short-term, bearish trend is three or more successive days in which the numbers are declining or are unchanged for one of the days. If it appears that a major trend is developing, temporary one- or two-day reversals in prices or the consensus will typically give you an opportunity to get aboard. A strong trend is indicated when the difference between successive daily consensus numbers is large and in one direction.

Extreme. An extreme Bullish Consensus number varies considerably with the specific futures. Historical data are your best sources of this information. Generally, the thinner the market, the greater the extremes. The numbers 5 and 95 are considered extreme in some of the thinly traded markets, whereas 30 and 70 are accepted as extremes in heavily traded markets.

Trades with Big Potential Profits

Trading opportunities for unusually big profits occur infrequently—maybe only once or twice a year, or not even that often in some futures. Consequently, patience is a required virtue.

The buy situation you are looking for is price testing and making only limited penetration into a major support area and the Bullish Consensus at historical lows. When such a situation occurs, you simply have to close your eyes and ears and buy—that is, take a contrary position. The ultimate confirmation that you are doing the right thing, which may not be available, would be bearish news and prices refusing to decline further. A sell is the reverse of this situation. Here the old saw is appropriate: "A market is always the most bullish at tops and most bearish at bottoms."

Using the Bullish Consensus with Your Trading System

In broad terms, you simply use the Bullish Consensus as a confirmation tool. Before taking a position using your present trading method, determine whether you would take the same position if you were using the Bullish Consensus as your basic trading tool. (See the prior section in this chapter on taking a position using only the Bullish Consensus.) If the two approaches to the market are not in accord, wait. You are likely to be money ahead by standing aside until you do get confirmation.

Some Trading Tips

1. Learn to be patient. Typically in a given commodity, there will be only a few big-profit, low-risk trades a year. Wait for what you believe to be the right opportunity.

2. Bulls die hard. Sharp rises in prices are more likely than sharp declines. A review of various bar charts will reveal that tops tend to be rounded, whereas bottoms tend to be somewhat sharp.

3. Trade with adequate funds in your account. They should be approximately five times the initial margin required for your position.

4. Forget the idea that you have to be on top of the market during the day. Following the market intraday is of value only to day traders.

5. Do not try to take a position within a few points of the bottom or the top. This is an exercise in futility, and you're likely to miss a major move.

6. Do not trade in a contract that is about to expire where significant liquidation is in process. Hedgers liquidating large positions can cause excessive volatility and unexpected price moves.

7. Be aware that some markets, such as foreign currencies and interest rates, are subject to unpredictable involvement by various governments.

Summing Up

So much information on the futures market is presented as a sure-fire prescription to instant wealth that it is appropriate to end this book on a downbeat. In theory, an accurate consensus is a perfect indicator, but its effectiveness is limited by the accuracy and timeliness of the numbers. Bear in mind:

1. A bullish situation can turn bearish in minutes, and vice versa, outdating currently available consensus numbers.

2. The Bullish Consensus is a poll of market advisors that market participants almost always follow, but there are rare exceptions, for example, the 1997–1998 stock market.

Also keep the following tips in mind:

1. Most speculators lose. Estimates range from 75 to 95 percent.

2. Most speculators are pitted against professionals, the locals on the floors of the exchanges, large speculators, and hedgers.

3. There is no Aladdin's Lamp in this business. Sure, you may be lucky over the short term, but long term, this is a tough game requiring lots of effort, skill, and intestinal fortitude. You'll earn every dollar!

4. The world and the markets are ever changing scenes, and so your trading strategies must be flexible enough to encompass these changes.

5. When your trading strategies are producing significant profits, you must trade heavily. As losing trades begin to mount, reduce the number of contracts traded. The market will grind down an even player in the same manner Las Vegas does.

6. Money management is a key element. Overconfidence will put you on the road to the poorhouse. Being certain that a specific price level will provide support or will not be broken, or vice versa, has been the downfall of many traders, including some of the biggies. Speaking from experience, this is a way to lose your shirt. No matter how confident you are that a specific price level will not be breached, when it occurs, tuck your tail between your legs, get out, accept your losses, and wait for your sanity to reassert itself.

7. Relatively few individuals have the psychological makeup required to be a really successful trader. Although this makeup is ill defined, one characteristic is the ability to plunge when a major market move is anticipated.

If you're still undaunted, then possibly, just possibly, futures trading is your game—its potential is unlimited.

Vegas pales beside the futures markets. Futures trading is the only game I know where one can start with as little as about $5,000 and run it up to a million or more in a matter of a few years or less. It takes a plunger who lives on the edge to do it, but it can be done. However, bear in mind that most people are not psychologically built to operate in this manner.

The next chapter provides charts and trading comments covering 24 different major futures. Rather than selecting just charts illustrating big winners, it was elected to provide Bullish Consensus charts that are likely to be encountered during any given seven-month period. As a reminder, big-profit, low-risk trades occur infrequently. Patience is not only a virtue—it is also a rewarding one.

Good luck and profitable trading!

Note

1. Historical Bullish Consensus data beginning in 1970 is available from Market Vane Corporation, P.O. Box 90490, Pasadena, CA 91109-0490. Phone (626) 395-7436, Fax (626) 795-7654, E-mail: marketvane@earthlink.net Web Site: marketvane.net

Chapter 10

MARKET SENTIMENT IN ACTION

The best is yet to come, because that's all there is.

— R. Earl Hadady

The charts presented in this chapter are courtesy of the *Bullish Consensus*, a weekly market letter published by Market Vane Corporation.[1] Daily updated consensus numbers on 33 futures markets are available from Market Vane. Simple daily price/consensus charts, such as these, will be your primary tool in using sentiment to trade.

To provide a representative sampling, the charts cover the same time period in 1998, with one exception. To include a low-risk, profitable trade in soybeans, the start date on this chart is March 30 as opposed to February 2.

Charts on the S&P 500, T-bonds, gold, crude oil, soybeans, and live cattle, the more widely traded commodities, have been included regardless of how well the Bullish Consensus performed. Charts on most of the other futures are also included.

As you review these charts, keep in mind what was stressed in earlier chapters. For a given futures, a low-risk, big-profit trade may occur only once or twice a year, and sometimes not even that frequently. However, this need not limit your trading because there are so many different futures from which to choose.

Typical parameters of a low-risk, big-profit, long side trade are a very low Bullish Consensus, say, around 15 or lower, and prices near the low of the past several months.

The parameters of a low-risk, big-profit, short side trade are a very high Bullish Consensus, say, about 85 or higher, and prices close to the high of the past several months. However, the risk for a short side trade is typically higher because tops tend to be more rounded, longer in duration, and more volatile as compared to bottoms. There is a saying, "Bulls die hard."

Typical low and high extremes in the Bullish Consensus vary from futures to futures, so it is necessary to have a framework for reference. For example, in a recent 12-month period, the consensus extremes in the S&P 500 were 29 and 81, whereas in soybeans they were 5 and 97. This information is provided each week in the market letter, *Bullish Consensus*.[1]

Another reminder: patience is a trader's best friend. Thinking that you must be in the market most of the time is a prescription for how to generate losses.

The lead-time of the Bullish Consensus versus price will vary with market conditions and the volatility of a particular futures. Even when there is no lead-time, the consensus provides valuable information. For example, if prices begin a sudden move, but the Bullish Consensus remains essentially unchanged, you can be reasonably sure that it is a false move. On the other hand, if the Bullish Consensus and prices are moving almost in sync, it is indicative that the price move is for real.

S&P 500

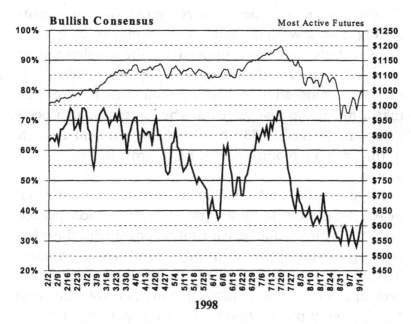

1998

The period covered includes an important high in the Dow, which occurred on July 17, 1998, when it closed above 9300, and the precipitous fall that followed.

The Bullish Consensus moved up in early February 1998 but then seesawed with lower highs and lower lows until the first part of June. This consensus action indicated that advisors were indecisive but as a group were turning increasingly bearish since each high was lower than the previous high. Meanwhile, the market was relatively steady. Keep in mind that the Bullish Consensus is derived from a poll of market advisors, whose advice is generally accepted and followed by the majority of traders and investors, but *not always*. This was a "not always" case: The public continued to pour money into the various mutual funds, and the fund managers had to put the money to work, which drove the market higher.[2] Finally, the advisors began to recognize what was happening and saw that their conventional trading tools were of little use. They jumped on the bandwagon in June and turned bullish until the top was reached. At that point, most advisors had the good sense to recognize that a major top was at hand. The consensus had been rising and peaked at 73 on July 16 but not near enough to the prior 12-month high of 81 to provide a strong sell signal.

There is little doubt that many traders incurred some heavy losses from being whipsawed before prices peaked in July. However, traders who got on board with the advisors, as a result of the steep drop in the consensus numbers, would have had super profits. But high profits were accompanied by high risks. The market volatility also required very nimble trading and deep pockets. A trader was better advised to look to other futures where lower-risk trades did exist during this period.

From its peak in mid-July, the consensus had been mostly in a free fall, and by mid-August it was approaching the prior 12-month low of 34. On August 31 the consensus had declined below the prior low; it bottomed at 29. When the consensus rose 5 points to 34 the next day, September 1, it was saying buy. A long position on the opening on September 2 could have been taken in the December contract at about 1010.50, very near the bottom.

This was not a market for the vast majority of traders, however. The daily volatility, high minus low, was running in the range of 20.00 to 40.00, 2,000 to 4,000 points. Although the consensus called out a buy near the bottom of this market, trading was best left to the professional hedgers.

There is no mistaking it: Everyone in the business, including the Bullish Consensus, found it tough calling the stock market during this period.

T Bonds

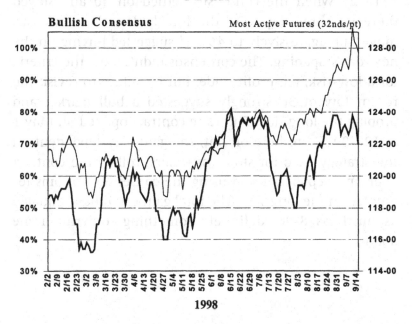

When the consensus declined steeply in mid-February, it appeared that it might approach or decline to the prior 12-month low of 29. The consensus touched 37 several times but refused to make a significant rally from there. On March 4, the consensus bottomed at 36 and was saying look to buy. By March 9, the consensus had risen to 45, a strong suggestion to go long. A buy on the opening on

March 10 could have been made in the June contract at 119-31. The consensus peaked at 66 on March 20 with prices above 121-00. The subsequent sharp decline in the consensus suggested an exit for a small profit or breakeven.

After exiting from the long position, the consensus trended lower and rallied in spurts. However, each rally fell short of the previous one. A bottom was reached on April 27 when the consensus settled on 40 and stayed there for three days. On the fourth day, the consensus moved up aggressively to 46 and suggested buying on the next day's opening. The consensus didn't meet the criteria for a low-risk, big-profit trade, but its failure to revisit the recent low of 36 strongly suggested a bull market and probing the long side. The June contract opened on May 1 at 120-09. From here on out, the gain was dependent on the strategy used for stop loss orders, rolling the contract over into September and using the consensus bottoms for reentry on the long side. The total gain could have equaled as much as 8-00, definitely something to write home about.

Market Sentiment in Action

Gold

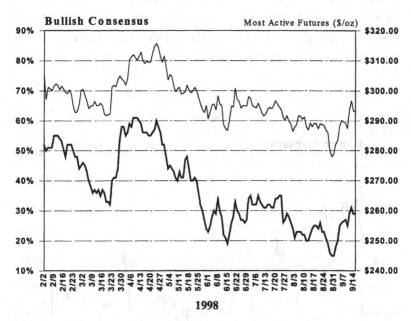

A review of this and other charts covering prior periods will reveal that the Bullish Consensus pretty much mirrored price action. Consequently, taking positions any time the consensus developed a trend of three days or more would have produced profits for a nimble trader. A good example was the strong rise in the consensus from its low of 32 on March 20. Prices in the June contract also soared from 293.80 on June 20 to $315.80 on April 23. About half of this rise of 22.00 should have been realizable.

There were no potential low-risk, big-profit trades until August 28 when the consensus dipped to 15, a new low, and sat there for two days. The prior 12-month low was 16. The consensus moved higher on September 1, and a buy on the opening of the 2 was indicated. Furthermore, prices were also at a low for the prior seven months. It proved to be a low-risk, profitable trade, but big profits failed to materialize. Half of the price rise of about 17.00 should have been achievable.

Silver

The rise of the Bullish Consensus above 80 in early February was an indication that the short side of the market should be considered. Moreover, a review of the prior 12 months revealed that the consensus had peaked in the 80s; prices had also begun to sag. Relative low-risk sales could have been executed at around $7.00. A significant rise in the consensus didn't occur until the end of February. Prices were also rising. These two indicators were saying that it was time to take profits and wait for the next signal.

112

An easy market exit in the $6.25 to $6.50 range was possible for a gain of about $0.65.

Through most of March, the consensus hovered around midrange, finally breaking above 55 and into the 60s. With the consensus finding support at midrange and finally turning up again, a bull market appeared to be present, an indication that later would prove to be erroneous. Trading with the consensus when it is bouncing around midrange can be risky business and is best left to day traders on the floor.

The next realistic signal occurred in April when prices were declining and the consensus high in late April failed to reach the prior high in early April. A somewhat risky sale could have been made around $6.00. With prices declining without any significant rallies, the sale could have been covered without difficulty around $5.25 for a gain of approximately $0.75.

Around June 1 the consensus approached 13, which was the low of the past 12 months. A low-risk buy was indicated. Although low risk, it turned out to be little more than a breakeven trade.

Subsequently, the yo-yoing consensus didn't provide any clear low-risk trades until the end of August when it dipped below 15. A low-risk buy could have been made at about $5.00 or less. In a highly volatile market, prices (off the chart) peaked at around $5.40 before the end of September, $0.40 above the entry.

Platinum

As compared to the heavily traded S&P 500, T Bonds, soybeans, and so on, several futures are relatively thinly traded; platinum, orange juice, and lumber, for example. As a result, fewer advisors follow or provide recommendations on these futures. Consequently, the consensus in these thinly traded and more volatile futures tends to reach higher and lower values. Values in excess of 90 and less than 10 are not uncommon. Keep this in mind when trading these futures.

The prior 12-month high and low in the consensus was 92 and 3. Consequently, the 70 reached in early February did not indicate a sufficiently overbought condition to consider a sale. However, the low of 15 in early March and the subsequent daily rise in the consensus suggested a high-risk buy could be considered. A long entry of around $390

114

could have been easily accomplished with an exit of about $410, when the consensus first peaked in the low 80s. The resulting gain was some $20.

The next trade signal came when the consensus breached 90, an indication of a highly overbought market. There was plenty of time to get off a sale about $410. Subsequently, the consensus dropped like a stone, and the steady decline in prices said stick with the short position. When the consensus dropped momentarily below 10, this was a signal to cover the short and go long. This position reversal could have been accomplished without difficulty around $360 for a gain of $50 on the short side.

After going long at about $360, the consensus rose and yo-yoed in the range of 10 to 20. However, each consensus high was higher than the prior high, and each low was higher than the previous low, presenting an encouraging sign. Sticking with the long side until the consensus dropped sharply and signaled an exit in mid-July, the position could have been liquidated near $390 for a gain of $30.

No reasonable-risk trades followed during the period charted.

Copper

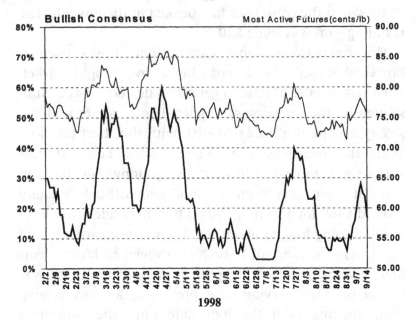

Bullish Consensus   Most Active Futures(cents/lb)

1998

When the consensus declined to about 11 and then rose to 15 in mid-February, a buy signal occurred. This signal proved to be premature, and depending on the resolution of the trader, a loss of around $2.50 could have been incurred.

The subsequent decline in the consensus below 10, particularly since the prior 12-month low was 11, was a clear recommendation to go long. A buy could have been made near $74.00. Other than a very minor decline of around $1.00, prices rose steadily and said stick with the long position; this was also confirmed by the consensus. When the consensus began to seesaw around the 50 level, it was an indication that it was time to take profits. An exit near the $82.00 level should have been easy to accomplish, resulting in a profit of about $8.00.

After the above trade when the consensus twice peaked in the range of 50 to 60, sales involved too much risk. However, in early April when the consensus dipped to 20 between the two peaks, a high-risk buy could have been made. The merit of such a buy was subsequently confirmed when the consensus marched steadily higher each day without so much as looking back. A buy was achievable around $78.00 and an exit near $84.00, a gain of some $6.00.

In mid-May through mid-July the consensus did its best to confound traders. For two months it seesawed while prices fortunately traded in a limited range, about $5.00. During this period, a nimble trader would have encountered small losses or small gains.

Finally, in early July the consensus dropped to an unbelievable low, less than 5. An unconditional low-risk buy was in order. A good rule to follow in such situations is to place an order to buy on the opening on the day after a significant rise occurs in the consensus. In this case, an entry near the low, about $72.50, would have been possible. Since prices rose steadily, but only to around $77.50, a gain of some $5.00 was possible; this was disappointingly small but nevertheless a gain.

Following this long side trade, the risk was too high for sales. However, in mid-August through the first of September, the low consensus said another buy was in order, but it was similar to the prior long side trade in which the gain was small.

Japanese Yen

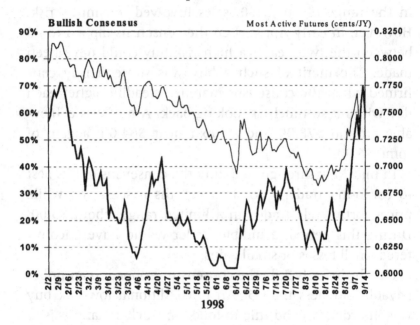

The high in the consensus of 71 was not a convincing sell signal; the consensus had reached 93 during the prior 12 months. However, the following and significant decline in the consensus numbers each day was a strong sell signal. But when sales aren't made off of an extreme, the risk is much higher. In this instance, the prices, which followed the consensus high, were very volatile, even as they declined. Ignoring the high risk, a nimble trader could have extracted considerable profit on the short side; a long term, deep pocket trader could have made a bundle.

A signal for the first low-risk trade occurred on April 3 when the consensus made a one-day low of 6 and subsequently began rising steadily. Going long in the June contract on the April 7 opening could have resulted in a buy at about 0.7570. However, any hoped-for large gain was not to be. A trader would have been fortunate to extract a gain of about $0.0125.

This scenario repeated itself about the first of June when a small loss would probably have been incurred.

By June 8 the consensus had dropped to the extreme low 2 where it remained for six straight days. On June 16 the consensus rose to 7, indicating that it was time to buy on the opening of the next market day, June 17. The market opened at 0.7065 and closed at 0.7428. It's hard to do better than that. A gain of 0.0300 should have been obtainable.

On August 3 the consensus dipped to 10, but it rose to 13 the following day. A buy in the September contract on the August 5 opening at about 0.6928 was possible. the low before prices lurched skyward was 0.6807, not too far below the entry price to be above a reasonable stop loss order. If the position was stopped out, another opportunity occurred on August 11 when the consensus dipped to 8 for one day. A buy in the September contract on the August 13 opening at 0.8865 was possible. From there, prices shot upward, and a profit of around 0.0700 should have been achievable.

Deutsche Mark

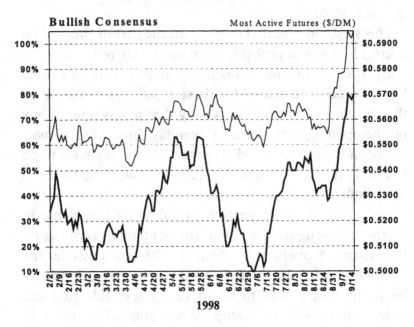

On March 5 the Bullish Consensus dipped to 15 and, with prices near lows dating back many months, it was a buy signal. A buy on the opening in the June contract at about 0.5498 was possible. This buy signal turned out to be around a month early. Either a small loss would have been incurred, or it would have been necessary to weather a price decline of 0.0089. Subsequently, a second, three-day bottom occurred in the consensus at 14. A buy on the opening in the June contract on April 2 at around 0.5432 would have been possible. In either case, a double top in the consensus in May said it was time to take profits and possibly turn to the short side. An exit around 0.5650 and a profit of about 0.0200 should have been obtainable.

A consensus low of 10 occurred on July 1. A buy signal occurred on July 6, the first market day the consensus rose

off of its low. On the opening on July 7, a buy could have
been made in the September contract at about 0.5542. The
low, which followed on July 10, was 0.5477, only 0.0065
below the entry, which should have been above any reasonable stop loss order. Prices in the September contract
peaked at 0.5956 so that a profit of at least 0.0300 should
have been achievable.

Swiss Franc

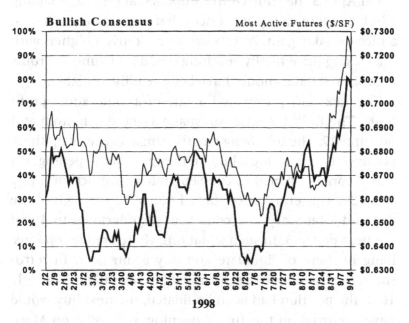

Based on criteria of a very low Bullish Consensus and
prices near a recent low, going long on March 10 was indicated. The consensus had declined to 4 on March 5 and
had remained there on Friday, March 6. Moreover, the
current low was essentially equal to the prior low of
0.6714 made on September 2, 1997. On Monday, March 9,

the consensus rose 4 points to 8 and was saying buy tomorrow. On March 10, the June contract opened at 0.6799. In the next several days, prices rose and peaked at 0.6865, tapering off after that. The consensus had risen to 17 before it, like prices, declined, finally bottoming at 6 on April 1. The long position entered at 0.6799 was doomed to be a small loser, probably about 0.0050.

An excellent low-risk, big-profit trade was available when the consensus made a one-day bottom at 6 on April 1. On April 3 the June contract opened at 0.6562, enabling a buy at about that price. Prices that day closed at 0.6613, a nice one-day gain. Afterward, prices moved higher, with the closing price finally reaching 0.6883 on June 4. Profits of around 0.0300 should have been readily available.

The next entry provided a one-of-a-kind, super-profit trade. The Bullish Consensus made a one-day bottom at 3 on June 29. The following day the consensus was up three points to 6, suggesting a buy on the next day's opening. On July 1, prices opened in the September contract for a buy at 66.29. This entry price turned out to be the high of the day and a bit scary; the consensus also declined to 4 and the next day to 3. In such situations, there are two options: hang in there or liquidate and buy again later. In retrospect, the low following the initial buy was 0.6503 on July 10. If the position had been liquidated, the next buy would have occurred on the July 7 opening at 0.6609; on Monday, July 6, the consensus had risen to 10 from a low of 3 on Thursday, July 2. The market was closed on Friday, July 3, for the July 4 holiday. Although gut wrenching at times, it is usually to the trader's advantage to maintain the initial position in such situations. As can be seen on the chart, prices moved steadily higher with only minor reactions until mid-August. Profits could have been taken at that time. Later, a higher-risk long position might have been entered on August 31 when the consensus was moving higher day-by-day. If the position had been retained, "this is good as it gets." The overall gain realized should have been about half or more of the move from roughly 0.6550 to 0.7250, some 0.0700.

British Pound

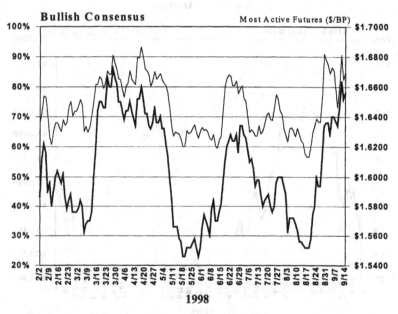

The consensus high for the prior 12 months was 92, and the low, 11. This immediately indicates that there were no low-risk trades during the period covered by the above figure.

At least four high-risk trades were available. These trades are identified by the consensus when it increases or decreases day-by-day without reversing direction for a period of several days, typically three or more days. The four most obvious of these opportunities came about on March 9, May 4, June 15, and August 17. There were other shorter periods, such as February 2. Let us repeat: futures trading at best is a high-risk business; trading in this manner makes it even riskier, but who can argue? Sometimes it's extremely profitable.

Canadian Dollar

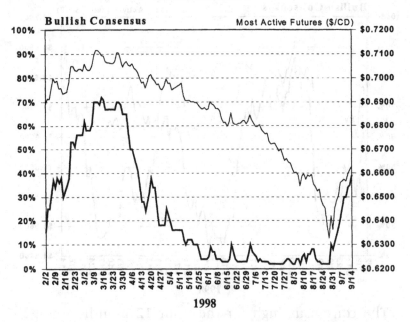

1998

Reviewing consensus data prior to the earliest date shown in the above chart, we see that, an extreme low of 4 occurred on January 29. Historical consensus data are invaluable and a must; they provide a reference for judging data range extremes for a specific futures.

Market Sentiment in Action

When the consensus dipped to 4 on January 29 (not on this chart) and rose the following day, a buy in the March contract could have been made when the market opened on February 2 at about $0.6906. If a close stop were used, an exit would have occurred on the mid-February dip, producing a small gain of about $0.0050. A more aggressive approach would have maintained the long position through the minor decline and produced a nice profit of about $0.0200. Reversing the position, from long to short, was also a good possibility.

The profit from the long position cited above was miniscule, however, compared to what an aggressive trader could have made. The prior 12-month consensus high was only 73, which suggested taking a short position when the consensus touched 72 in the middle of March. The earlier long position was also liquidated at about this time, so this position could have been reversed. The price rally toward the end of March was worrisome, but the consensus said not to be concerned; its high of 70 failed to equal the prior high of 72. From here on in, particularly during June, it was primarily a question of hanging in through minor price rallies and three consensus rallies that lasted only two or three days. At worst, a handsome profit would have been made; at best, a fantastic profit was possible.

A buy signal occurred in early September. The consensus rose from a low of 2 on August 27 to 17 on September 3. Furthermore, an upside breakout was signaled when the consensus rose above 10, its three prior highs. A buy could have been made in the December contract at about 0.6493 on the September 4 opening. By September 16 the high had reached 0.6658, so more than 0.0100 in profit should have been available.

Crude Oil

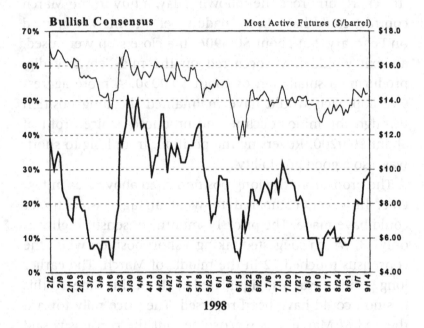

After declining in February and March, the Bullish Consensus bottomed at 5 on March 9, testing the prior 12-month low of 4. The next day's rally to 9 suggested a buy on the following day's opening. The May contract opened at 14.59 on March 11, and a buy could have been executed near this price. Following this entry, the consensus held at 9 and then dipped to 4 on March 17. Prices also hit a low of 13.15. As explained in an earlier analysis, there are two options in such situations: hang in there or liquidate and go long on the next buy signal. This next buy signal came when the consensus made a one-day bottom at 4 on March 17 and rose 10 points the next day. On March 19, prices opened at 14.53 in the May contract, as opposed to the initial buy at 14.59. Although it's tough, it is usually

126

to the trader's advantage to maintain the initial position in such situations. On March 26, prices in the May contract hit a high of 17.20 with a close of 16.83. About half of the difference between the entry and the high close, roughly 1.30, should have been captured as profit. Though not a great trade, it was acceptable.

The next trade opportunity occurred on June 15 when the consensus made a one-day bottom at 4. A buy on the opening on June 17 was possible around 13.35 in the August contract. After making a low of 13.06 following the entry, prices marched higher to produce a nice profit.

On August 11 the consensus dropped to 5 and stayed there two days before moving significantly higher. A buy was indicated on the August 14 opening; the November contract opened at 13.87. Before moving higher, the November contract made a low of 13.32, but by the end of September, it was trading around 16.00 to produce a nicely profitable trade.

Heating Oil

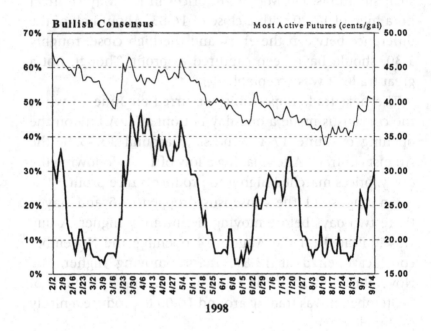

A review of the consensus data prior to the first date shown on the above chart reveals a prior high of 83 on October 3 in 1997. This establishes a consensus extreme, an approximate level at which a low-risk sale can be considered. For the period covered in the chart, there are no such short position opportunities. The failure of the consensus to even reach midrange, 50, indicates that this futures is in a bear market. It also says be wary of the long side.

Looking at consensus data prior February 2 puts the prior low at 3 in late January 1998. Since this futures is in a bear market and the consensus low was quite recent, extra care should be exercised before taking a long position. Taking a long position prior to the consensus touching its prior low would, with a close stop, have produced a small loss.

Waiting for the consensus on March 9 to touch its prior low of 3 before going buying would have produced a profit of about $5.00. Similar situations occurred in late May, early June, and August.

When the consensus keeps flirting with very low numbers, one should wait for the first consensus high to be exceeded before taking a long position. This rule-of-thumb will at least minimize losses and produce some profits most of the time.

Gasoline, Unleaded

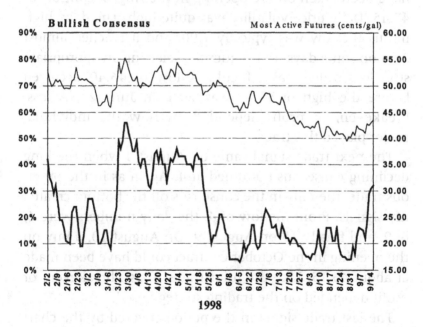

Historically, the prior 12-month consensus low was 3. This low occurred from January 21 through January 23 in

1998, about two weeks before the first date shown on this chart. Consequently, the February and March consensus lows, which barely got below 10, shouldn't have been considered as signals to consider going long. The lack of any clear direction in prices also confirmed this view. After peaking at 56 on March 26, the consensus turned lower, an indication that gasoline was in a bear market.

The first trade signal came on June 15 when the consensus hit bottom at 3, matching the prior 12-month low. The next day the consensus rose only 2 points to 5, an iffy buy signal. When in doubt, one should wait. The following day the consensus was up 5 to settle on 10, a clear buy indication. On the following day, June 18, a long position could have been taken on the opening in the August contract at 47.45. Daily price volatility was quite high. The daily high minus the low was typically 1.00, and it reached almost 2.00 on some days. Consequently, selecting an appropriate stop loss order was difficult. A low of 46.40 occurred before the high of 49.35 was seen on June 23. A loss, breakeven, or profit depended on how the individual trader played this trade.

The next trade signal came on August 3 when the long declining consensus bottomed at 4. Again as in the previous trade, the rally in the consensus off the bottom created iffy signals. From the low of 4, the daily numbers were 6, 6, 9, and finally 15 on August 9. On August 10, a buy on the opening in the October contract could have been made at about 43.15. Like the prior trade, a loss, breakeven, or profit depended on the trading strategy used.

The last trade signal in the period covered by the chart occurred on August 27 when the consensus bottomed at 4. After remaining on 4 for two more days, it moved up 5 points to 9. A buy could have been made in the November contract on the September 2 opening at 41.45. The low of 40.80 was also made that same day; afterward, prices never looked back until a high of 47.80 was made on October 1, 6.35 above the buy price. This example was very close to an ideal consensus trade, but keep in mind you're in the real world. There are also going to be some losers, hopefully small ones.

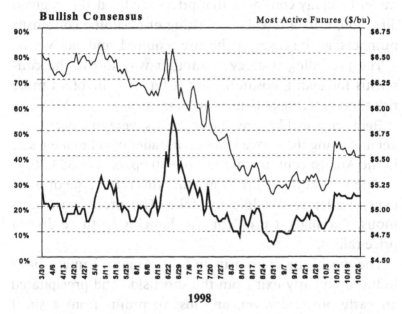

Soybeans

Bullish Consensus   Most Active Futures ($/bu)

1998

There was a big-profit trade the week of June 22, but it couldn't be classified as low-risk. Extending this chart back two months showed prices in a steady down trend; each successive high was lower than the prior one. The bear market was confirmed during the later part of June when the Bullish Consensus couldn't rise above midrange.

Moreover, the consensus June 24 high of 55 was less than the February 9 high of 57, not shown on this chart—a case of successive lower highs.

Following the June 24 consensus high of 55, the next two daily numbers were 52 and 49; this was a strong indication to go short, suggesting that prices are going to move a lot lower. The number of successive down days in the consensus that are used to enter the market is a judgment call. Normally, the number of days used should be related to one's confidence in the market's overall direction. If a trader is highly confident that prices are headed in a given direction, only a few days of rising or declining consensus numbers, as the case may be, are required, and vice versa.

The preceding strategy is another way to use the consensus for taking positions, but it typically involves more risk than entering at consensus extremes.

Being reasonably sure that soybeans were in a bear market and using the above strategy, a trader could make a sale in the August contract on the June 30 opening at 653.50.

One look at the chart shows that this is the type of trade every trader would like to make. The profit was enormous. The biggest problem was hanging in there during price rallies.

The dip of the consensus to 8 on August 7 might have induced an early exit from the short side and precipitated an early buy. However, any loss of profits from a short position, or any loss on a subsequent long position, would have been replaced by the low-risk, profitable buy signal in early September. On August 31 the consensus bottomed at 5; the next day it was up 2, an iffy buy signal; the next day it was up 3, so a buy was in order the next day. On September 3, prices opened in the November contract at

520.25. It was only necessary to weather a low about 5.00 below the entry price; the November contract went off the boards at 579.00. Trades don't get much better than this.

Wheat

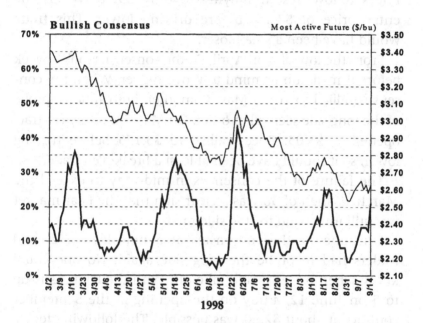

Wheat futures had been in a decline since September 1997. The consensus had ranged from a high of 80 to a low of 7 during the 12 months prior to the first date on the chart. Consequently, the dip in the consensus to 10 in early March stirred only a little interest in considering a long position. Moreover, the subsequent inability of the consensus to rise to even 40 was a strong indicator that the bear market was still intact.

The consensus declined to 6 on April 3 but failed to rally more than two points until April 9 when an up trend developed; the consensus numbers were 7 on April 9, 9 on April 13, and 11 on April 14. On April 15, the July contract opened at $3.15, enabling a buy near that price. The consensus moved up to 14 on the entry day and stayed there for three days before finally tailing off to 4 on April 27. Prices followed suit, rallying to only $3.18, versus the entry price of $3.15, before drifting lower. This trade would have been a small loser.

From the low of 4 on April 27, the consensus took a week before it made up its mind to move higher. When the consensus rallied to 10 on May 4, another, but cautious, probe of the long side seemed in order. On May 5 the July contract opened at $3.05. Prices rallied to $3.175 before turning lower, so it should have been at least a breakeven trade.

The failure of the consensus in mid-May to exceed the March 17 high of 36 was a clear sign that the bear market was still intact and to stay sidelined.

On June 11 the consensus, at a new low of 2, said traders had to probe the long side again. No one could know when prices would take off. With the consensus up to 5 on June 12, a buy on the opening in the September contract at about $2.90 was possible. The following feeble rally only made it up to $3.065 before prices again tumbled. At best, this trade would have broken about even.

The consensus peaked at 43 on June 24, failing to reach even midrange; a precipitous decline followed. Both events confirmed that the bear market was still intact. The consensus numbers from the high on successive days were 43, 40, 37, and 29. Going short was somewhat risky, but in view of the prior long-term bearish cast, it was not unreasonable. A sale on the June 30 opening in the September contract could have been made at $2.81. The high that followed was only $2.92, so a stop loss $0.10 above the entry would have protected this very good trade. In the last half of July, the yo-yoing of the consensus between 6 and 10 was cause for concern, but prices never rallied significantly. On August 6 and 7 the low in the September contract was $2.46. The spread between the entry price and the low was $0.35; an astute trader should have been able to convert at least half of this move into profits.

When the consensus bottomed at 7 on August 3 and subsequently rose to 10, then 11, and finally 13 on August 10, it was a signal to probe the long side again. On August 11, the December contract opened at $2.725. The rally that followed reached $2.81, and the consensus topped out at 25 on August 17 before the bears again took control. The consensus suggested an exit on August 24 when it declined to 15 on the previous day. This was at best a breakeven trade, probably a small loser.

The next trade signal came on August 31 when the consensus dipped to 4 for two days. However, another long side probe shouldn't have been considered until the consensus rallied above 10, the level that it had been unable to surmount on July 14, 20, and 31. On September 8, the consensus had reached 14 and appeared headed higher. A buy on the September 9 opening in the December contract could have been made at about $2.655. The high in the December contract topped out at $3.01 on October 26. At least half of the $0.35 rise in prices should have been convertible into profits, certainly not a trade to knock. This trade illustrates why each and every consensus signal must be probed. There is no way to tell which trade is going to be the big one, but you can be reasonably sure that any losers are going to be small.

Live Cattle

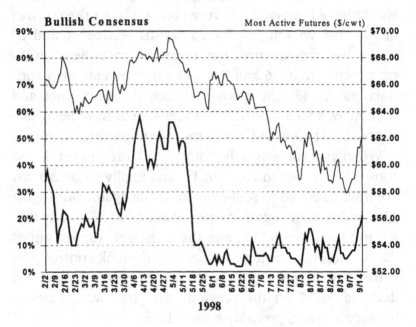

1998

The first potential buy occurred on February 10 when the consensus dipped to 11; the prior 12-month low was 8, only 3 points lower. The consensus rose to 16 the follow-ing day, suggesting a buy on the opening the next day. On February 12, April cattle opened at 66.60. The following days saw cattle prices move higher, peaking at 68.25 on February 17. An agile trader would have picked up about half of the rally of 1.65; at worst, he would have broken even.

The next trade alert came on February 19 when the consensus dipped to 10, where it stayed for three days. On February 24, the consensus rose 4 points to 14, suggesting a buy on the next day's opening. Taking a long position around 66.00 in the June contract should have been possi-ble on February 24. Prices only closed below the entry price one day—the day after the buy was made and then, only by a few points. It was mostly downhill from there and hanging in during price setbacks. The consensus looked back only once, when it dipped to the prior consensus high of 21. In the June contract, prices peaked above 69.00. At least half of the 3.00 move should have been convertible into profit. This wasn't a great trade but better than a poke in the eye with a sharp stick.

In April and early May, the inability of the Bullish Consensus to rise above midrange, 40–60, was a strong indication that this was a bear market. Furthermore, the May consensus high of 56 fell short of the earlier April high of 58. These were signals to look to the short side. Although the following trade produced significant profits, it is not one that the Bullish Consensus would normally recommend. However, it does illustrate what a very aggressive trader can do using the consensus.

A strong down trend in the consensus developed after the May 4 high of 56; on successive days the numbers were 56, 54, 51, and 46. However, the low in the consensus didn't drop below the prior low of 39 in mid-April, which said wait until this low is taken out. This occurred on May 14 when the consensus dipped to 33 and continued to move lower on successive days: 33, 25, and 12. Although an iffy and risky trade, particularly with the consensus moving into such low numbers, a sale could have been made on the May 18 opening at 67.85 in the August contract. By early August, prices had dropped below 58.00, which made a handsome profit possible if the position had been held through price rallies and the worrisome low, nontrending, and erratic consensus numbers.

Buying off of the consensus lows that occurred in June and July would have resulted in a series of losses.

Using the ultra low consensus of 2 on August 3 would have produced a small profit.

When the consensus dipped to 5 on September 2 and 3, it was an alert to be ready to probe the buy side again. A buy was in order when the consensus rallied to 11 on September 10. On September 11, the December contract opened at 62.70; a long position could have been established near that price. Following this entry, price ranged between a low of 61.50 and a high above 66.00. A profit of at least 01.50 should have been garnered from this trade.

Pork Bellies

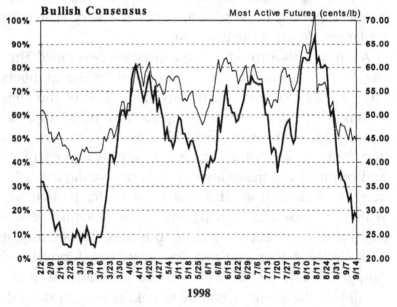

As February progressed, the consensus continued to decline. Reviewing past data showed that the consensus had dipped to a low of 6 during the prior 12 months, a level around which a buy should be undertaken. A low of 5 did occur on February 20 and 23, so a buy order should have been placed on the morning following the first day the consensus rose, which was February 25. On February 26 a long position could have been established in the May contract when it opened at $41.35. Subsequently, the consensus yo-yoed a bit until the middle of March before surging higher. Meanwhile, prices, with only minor retracements, moved steadily higher until $60.00 was reached. The consensus also moved higher until it reached 81 on April 9, which was considerably short of 94, the prior 12-month high. From 81, the consensus dropped precipitously to 74 and then to 70, indicating it was time to take profits and exit. Liquidation could have been accomplished near the April 15 opening at $58.40. From the entry price of $41.35, this is a gain of about $17.00, half of which should have been convertible into a nice profit.

The next entry alert came in the middle of August when bellies were up and down the limit. On August 14 the consensus hit 93, and it looked like it might take out the prior 12-month high of 94. On the following market day, prices were down the limit; the consensus also tanked. It was stand aside time and wait for the smoke to clear. The next day, August 18, prices recovered practically all of the prior day's limit-down loss (not apparent on the chart). The consensus was also up 2 points. The next day, August 19, the consensus was down 4 points to 80, a signal to sell the next day. August 20 was test-your-courage day; sales in the February contract on the opening could have been made without trouble around $56.00. Other than a rally on the entry day, which saw a high of $57.40, it was all down hill. On September 1, prices in the February contract hit a low of $42.45. This was a price decline of $13.55 from the entry price, at least half of which could have been converted into profit. It can get better that this—but not by much.

Sugar

If around the first of April consideration was being given to trading sugar, the first entry alert occurred when the consensus dipped to 11 on April 17. The low and high for the consensus during the prior 12 months were 14 and 97, respectively. The consensus rose the next day to 14, so a buy was in order the next market day, April 21. The July sugar contract opened at 8.94, and the consensus was up another notch to 16. However, the rally in both prices and the consensus fizzled, and by April 27 the consensus had declined to 5, where it rested for three days. Prices had declined to approximately the entry price, making this about a breakeven trade.

On April 30 the consensus moved up 3 points from 5, which suggested probing the long side the next day. Prices in the July contract opened at 8.37 on May 1. Following the entry, prices rose steadily to peak at 9.45 on May 12. This was not a big gain but sufficient to provide an acceptable profit of about half of the 1.08 increase in prices. The consensus peaked two days later at 48 before it began a steady decline.

The next trade alert occurred on June 15 when the consensus dropped to a new low, 4. It rested at 4 for two days but rose to 10 on June 17. This was a signal to buy the next day. On June 18, October sugar opened at 8.27 to enable a buy at about this price. After a price retreat to a low of 7.94, prices developed an up trend and rose to peak at 9.11 on August 11. About half of the price rise of 1.17 could have been converted into a profit.

The dip in the consensus to 5 on September 11 was an alert to again probe the long side. Checking beyond the last date of this chart, we see that prices were relatively flat. A consensus trade in mid-September would have resulted in either a small loss or a gain.

Cocoa

Taking a look at Cocoa in early February, we see that a long position appeared to be in the offing as the consensus continued to decline almost daily. The records show the prior 12-month consensus low to have been 11; the present trend suggested that the low might be repeated. However, when the consensus declined to 14 on February 12 but turned up the following day, it was time to buy on the next market day's opening at about $1,560. Prices rose steadily higher with only minor reactions, but the consensus began to yo-yo throughout March, which suggested it was time to consider liquidating the long position. An exit at about $1,625 should have been easy, producing a profit of $65.

Prices and the consensus dropped precipitously in mid-April to bottom on February 14 and 15. Trading at this time involved considerable risk, and the sidelines seemed like the place to be. However, a nimble trader would have made out nicely using the rule-of-thumb of going with the consensus when it advanced or declined for three or four consecutive days.

The next trade opportunity came on June 15 when the consensus declined and held at 15 for two days before turning up to 17. On the following day, a long could have been initiated at $1,602, but this would have been a loser because prices declined sufficiently, about 30 or 300 actual dollars, to hit a reasonable stop loss order.

Four market days later, the consensus suggested another buy when it rose to 17 after setting on 14 for three days. This consensus signal turned out to be valid but would have produced only a small profit.

Having experienced earlier consensus numbers of 14, 15, and 14, the 14 that occurred on August 3 was enough to make one view another long with trepidation. However, not knowing when the big winner is going to come along, the trader must check out every consensus extreme. This long would have turned out to be a small winner or loser, depending on the stop.

As August progressed, the consensus again dipped to 14 on August 17 and 18, the prior low. Assuming a buy on the opening on August 20, prices declined $48, which would have triggered a reasonable stop and generated a loss.

Later, on August 24 and 25, the consensus hit a new low of 11, testing a trader's perseverance to go long. This trade finally paid some dividends. From an opening-price entry on August 27, prices rose some $61 before turning lower, thus enabling some profits. At best, trading cocoa during this period turned out to be educational but clearly nothing to write home about.

Cotton

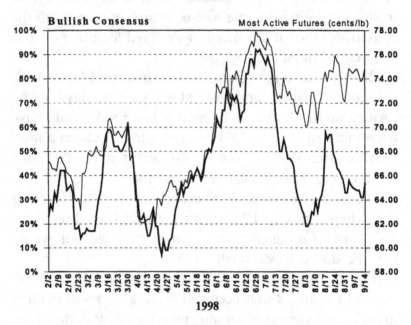

Considering a trade in cotton in early February, the prior 12-month low of 3 in the consensus said stay sidelined for the time being. After rising to around 40, the consensus declined steeply until it had dropped below 20. Whether to consider probing the long side at this juncture is a judgment call. "Wait and see" is usually good advice in such instances. Several consecutive up days in the consensus, three, for example, is usually a strong indication that a buy is in order. This strategy is usable throughout the entire consensus range, but the risk increases as it moves away from a low or high extreme. In this case, the consensus dawdled seven days before it rose three consecutive days: 17, 24, and 30. On March 10, a buy could have been made in the May contract on the opening at approximately 68.20. The consensus moved up steadily, peaking at 59;

144

closing prices peaked at the same time at 70.74. When the consensus started to decline, liquidation of the long May at about 70.00 for a gain of 1:80 shouldn't have been difficult.

The next consensus buy alert came when it dipped to 15 on April 7. This seemed to be a valid buy signal because the consensus declined to within 1 point of the prior buy signal back in February. On April 15, the consensus rose off of its low, and a buy was in order on the opening of the following market day, April 16, at 65.00 in the July contract. This is about as good as it gets. Prices took off higher and rarely looked back; reactions were small. There was a scary drop in the consensus when it dipped to 7 on April 22, but it was negated by the strong surge in prices.

Exiting from this great trade would depend on the particular strategy used by an individual trader. On June 8 the consensus hit 76, 4 above the prior 12-month high of 72. Prices broke the next day, June 9, when they were almost limit down. The following day prices were only down 0.65, so, at worst, an exit of about 73.00 could have been made, resulting in a gain of 8.00. The next day prices resumed their upward move. The consensus declined for only two days before it rallied and began to vacillate. Reversing and going short at this juncture was a possibility, which if elected would have resulted in a small loss. If the position were held through the next price and consensus surge, an exit at around 75.00 was reasonable for a gain of 10.00. The consensus peaked at 92 on June 29 with the first significant decline of 4 occurring on July 6. A position reversal or sale could have been made in the December contract at 76.15 on the opening on July 7. From there, it was all downhill again. There was only a one-day, 5-point blip in the consensus on July 17, before it moved lower or was unchanged each day. It bottomed at 19 on August 3. By August 6, the consensus had risen to 25 and was saying take profits. Reversing the position was judged too risky because the consensus didn't decline to approximately its previous lows. An exit on the opening of August 7 could have been made in the December contract at 73.15, producing a profit of 3.00.

Lumber

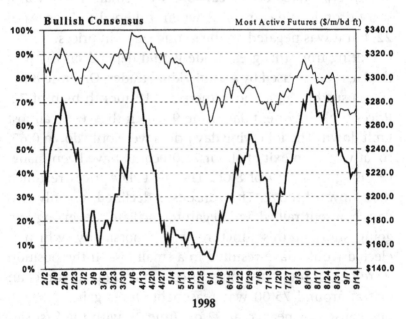

Beginning in February, the consensus was just below midrange and saying, stand aside, wait for an extreme to be reached. The prior 12-month high and low had been 93 and 3.

As weeks passed, the consensus swung between 10 and 76 until the end of May when it declined below 10 and a trade alert seemed in the offing. The consensus refused to rally more than 1 point until the low of 4 was reached on June 1. On June 3 the consensus rose 3, signaling that a buy was in order on the opening the next day, June 4. A long position could have been entered in the July contract at about $270.00. Prices rose, with typical reactions of 50 percent or less, until closing prices finally peaked at 292.90. Meanwhile, the consensus moved higher to peak at 56 on June 29, rarely backtracking more than one or two points, and then only for one or two days. On July 6, when the consensus dropped 6 points, it was a signal to take profits on the opening the next market day. On July 7, the July contract opened at 287.90, resulting in a gain of about 17.00.

A subsequent trade involving higher risk was indicated when the consensus bottomed sharply on July 16 at 22. Closing prices also bottomed on this day. Other than a 2-point setback, the consensus rose strongly to 33 (11 points) by July 21. A buy on the opening on July 22 could have been made in the September contract at 285.80. Prices rose without any significant reactions and closed at 315.20 on August 6, the top. The consensus was less than helpful in ascertaining when to exit. However, when the consensus dropped to 64 from 72 on August 17, the September long could have been liquidated on the August 18 opening at 298.00 for a gain 12.50.

Notes

1. Market Vane Corporation, P.O. Box 90490, Pasadena, CA 91109-490, Phone (626) 395-7436, Fax (626) 795-7654. E-mail: marketvane@earthlink.net. Web Site: marketvane.net
2. R. Earl Hadady, "Mutual funds flow sinks bear market," *Futures*, June 1997, p. 30.

GLOSSARY

The definitions provided herein apply to the futures markets. They may have other meanings when used in a different context.

Accumulate (accumulation). The act of adding to a futures position over a period of time, usually at predetermined time intervals and/or price levels.

Acreage allotment. The number of acres a farmer can plant to a given crop under a voluntary farm program and still receive the benefits of government price supports and financial assistance; acreage established under the federal farm program to stimulate production of certain crops of limited supply and curtail production of others in ample supply; an aspect of the large acreage diversion policy of the farm program.

Acreage reserve. An acreage that is part of the acreage allotment for which a farmer can receive government payment for not planting a given crop.

Actuals. The physical or cash commodity, as distinguished from commodity futures contracts.

Afloat. Commodities in harbor or in transit on vessels.

Arbitrage. The simultaneous purchase of one commodity against the sale of another in order to profit from distortions from usual price relationships. Variations include simultaneous purchase and sale of different delivery months of the same commodity, of the same commodity and delivery month on two different exchanges, and purchase of one commodity against the sale of another commodity. See also Spread and Straddle.

Back spreading. Buying distant (back) delivery months versus selling a contract month having an earlier delivery date; a bear spread. Theoretically, this type of spread involves unlimited risk.

Basis. (1) in the strict sense, the difference between the cash or spot price and the price of the nearest futures contract; (2) price basis—as in "price basis Chicago"— agreement between buyer and seller that the price for a transaction will be based on the cash price at a given location, at a given time. Sometimes the word "basis" is used synonymously with "cash commodity" as in the phrases "long the basis" or "short the basis," meaning that one has bought or sold the cash commodity.

Bear. A trader who is expecting prices to decline.

Bearish. An opinion or condition that favors lower prices.

Bear spread. A spread in which the long position is in the more distant contract month.

Bid. An offer to buy a specific quantity of a commodity at a stated price.

Board of Trade. Chicago Board of Trade. See CBOT.

BOT. Short for Chicago Board of Trade. See CBOT.

Break. A sudden and unexpected decline in market prices.

Breakout. A price move, either above or below the range of prices where trading has been taking place, which usually determines the future trend of prices for an appreciable time period, that is, a week or more. This term is more often used when prices break out on the up side.

Broker. (1) A person paid a fee or commission for acting as an agent in making contracts or sales; (2) floor broker—in commodities futures trading, a person who actually executes orders on the trading floor of an exchange; (3) account executive—the person who deals with customers and their orders in commission house offices. See also Registered commodity representative.

Brokerage. A fee charged by a broker for execution of a transaction; an amount per transaction or a percentage of the total value of the transaction; usually referred to as a commission fee.

Brokerage house (or firm). A company that buys and sells futures contracts to commodity customers for a fee.

Bucket, bucketing. Illegal practice of accepting orders to buy or sell without executing such orders, and the illegal use of the customer's principal and/or margin deposit without disclosing the fact of such use.

Bulge. A strong advance in futures or cash prices.

Bull. A trader who is expecting prices to advance.

Bullish. An opinion or condition that favors higher prices.

Bull market. A market in which the price trend for an extended period, typically a month or more, is higher.

Bull spread. A spread in which the short position is in the more distant contract month.

Butterfly spread. A spread using three different and

consecutive contract months in which the contract month of the short position is between the contract months of the two long positions, or vice versa.

Buy in.   A purchase to cover a previous sale, often called short covering. See also Cover.

Buying hedge (or long hedge).   Buying futures contracts to protect against a possible rise in the price of the commodity at some specific date in the future. See also Hedging.

Buy on close or opening.   To buy at the end or the beginning of the trading session at a price within the closing or opening range of prices.

Buy on stop.   A market order to buy when and if prices rise and touch a specified price. Order is used principally as a stop loss order for a short position or to enter the market on the long side when and if prices break out on the upside above a resistance level.

C&F.   Cost and freight paid to port of destination or cost and freight of shipping a commodity.

CBOT.   Chicago Board of Trade, 141 West Jackson Boulevard, Chicago, IL 60604, Phone (312) 435-3620, Fax (312) 341-3306.

CFTC.   Commodity Futures Trading Commission. A federal regulatory agency established in 1974 charged with responsibility for regulating futures trading.

CIF. Cost, insurance, and freight of shipping a commodity.

CME. Chicago Mercantile Exchange, 30 South Wacker Drive, Chicago, IL 60606, Phone (312) 930-1000, Fax (312) 930-3439.

COMEX. Commodity Exchange Inc., 4 World Trade Center, New York, NY 10048, Phone (212) 938-2900, Fax (212) 321-9458.

CPO. Commodity Pool Operator.

CRCE. Chicago Rice & Cotton Exchange, 141 West Jackson Boulevard, Chicago, IL 60604, Phone (312) 341-3078, Fax (312) 347-3827.

CSCE. Coffee, Sugar & Cocoa Exchange Inc., 4 World Trade Center, New York, NY 10048, Phone (212) 938-2800, Fax (212) 524-9863.

CTA. Commodity Trading Advisor.

Call. (1) A period in which the price for each futures contract is established, that is, an opening or a closing call; (2) buyers' call—a purchase of a specified quantity of a specific grade of a commodity at a fixed number of points above or below a specified delivery month in futures, with the buyer being allowed a certain period of time within which to fix the price by either purchasing a future for the account of the seller or indicating to the seller when he or she wishes to fix price; (3) seller's call—same as the buyer's call except that the seller has the right to determine the time to fix price; (4) a term applied to an option to buy a futures contract or other security at a specified price within a given time period.

Cargo. A commodity loaded aboard ship. A cargo of grain is typically 350,000 bushels.

Carload. A commodity loaded aboard a railway car. A carload of grain is typically about 2,000 bushels.

Carrying charges (or costs). (1) Those costs incurred in warehousing the physical commodity, generally including interest, insurance, and storage; (2) "full carrying charge market"—a situation in the futures market when the price difference between delivery months reflects the full costs of interest, insurance, and storage.

Carrying charge spread. A spread in which the nearby contracts sell at a discount to the more distant contracts. The risk in such spreads is usually limited to the cost of carrying the commodity, that is, storage, insurance, and interest charges.

Carryover. That part of current supplies of a commodity comprised of stocks from previous production/marketing seasons.

Cash commodity. Actual stocks of a commodity as distinguished from futures contracts; goods available for immediate delivery or delivery within a specified period following sale; or a commodity bought or sold with an agreement for delivery at a specified future date. See also Actuals and Forward contracting.

Cash forward sale. See Forward contracting.

Cash price. The price that the commodity is trading for in the cash markets.

Certificated stock. Stocks of a commodity that have been inspected and found to be of a quality deliverable against futures contracts, stored at the delivery points designated as regular or acceptable for delivery by the commodity exchange.

Charting. The use of graphs and charts in the technical analysis of futures markets to plot prices, trends or price movements, average movements of price, and volume and open interest. See also Technical analysis.

Chicago Board of Trade. See CBOT.

Churning. Unnecessary transactions in a customer's account generated by an unscrupulous broker for the sake of producing extra commissions; an action usually subject to legal redress.

Clearinghouse. An agency connected with commodity exchanges through which all futures contracts are made, offset, and fulfilled through delivery of the actual commodity, and through which financial settlement is made; is often a fully chartered separate corporation rather than a division of the exchange proper.

Clearing member. A member of an exchange who is also a member of the clearinghouse associated with the exchange; has financial responsibilities beyond a regular exchange member.

Clearing price. Used interchangeably with settlement price. See Settlement price.

Closing price or range. A price or range of closely related prices at which transaction took place at the closing of the market; buying and selling orders at the closing might have been filled at any point with such a range. See also Settlement price.

Commission. The fee charged to a customer by a broker for executing a futures transaction.

Commission house. See Futures commission merchant.

Commission merchant. See Futures commission merchant.

Commitment of Traders Report. A report issued periodically by the Commodity Futures Trading Commission (CFTC). The report reveals the market composition, that is, the proportion of the market held by different types of traders on a specific date.

The types of traders are classified by the CFTC as hedgers (often referred to as commercials), spreaders, large speculators, and small speculators. The specific number of traders, other than small speculators, is also provided.

Commodity Credit Corporation (CCC). An agency of the U.S. government established in 1933. Its purpose is to stabilize, support, and protect farm income and prices, to assist in maintaining balanced and adequate supplies of agricultural commodities and their products, and to facilitate the orderly distribution of commodities.

Commodity Exchange Authority (CEA). A former regulatory agency (replaced by the Commodity Futures Trading Commission in 1974) of the U.S. Department of Agriculture set up to administer the Commodity Exchange Act, which supervised trading on commodity exchanges regulated as contract markets. See also Grain Futures Act.

Commodity Futures Trading Commission. See CFTC.

Commodity pool operator (CPO) An individual or organization that operates or solicits funds for a commodity pool—that is, an enterprise in which funds contributed by a number of persons are combined for the purpose of trading futures contracts or commodity options. A CPO generally must register with the CFTC.

Commodity representative. See Registered commodity representative.

Commodity Trading Advisor (CTA) A person who, for compensation or profit, directly or indirectly advises others as to the value of or the advisability of buying or selling futures contracts or commodity options. A CTA generally is required to register with the CFTC.

Contango. A British term referring to a carrying charge market.

Contract. A bilateral agreement between the buyer and seller in a futures transaction. Also refers to a unit of the commodity being traded.

Contract grades. Standards or grades of commodities listed in the rules of the exchanges which must be met when delivering cash commodities against futures contracts. Grades are often accompanied by a schedule of discounts and premiums allowable for delivery of commodities of lesser or greater quality than the contract grade.

Contract month. The month in which a given futures contract matures, and delivery and acceptance of the commodity is made.

Contrarian. A trader whose opinion on future market prices is opposite to the opinion shared by the majority of traders.

Glossary

Contrary opinion. An opinion that is opposite to the sentiment held by the majority; for example, if 80 percent of the traders in a given market were bullish, a bearish view would be a contrary opinion.

Controlled account. An arrangement by which the holder of the account gives written power of attorney to another, often his broker, to make buying and selling decisions without notification to the holder; also referred to as a managed account or a discretionary account.

Corner. (1) To secure such relative control of a commodity or security that its price can be manipulated; (2) in the extreme, to obtain more contracts requiring the delivery of commodities or securities than the quantity of such commodities or securities actually in existence.

Cover. To offset a previous futures transaction with an equal and opposite transaction; usually refers to offsetting (closing out) a short position taken at an earlier date. Offsetting (closing out) a long position taken at an earlier date is usually referred to as liquidation. See also Liquidation and Short covering.

Crop report. A U.S. Department of Agriculture report covering the state of a commodity or commodities.

Crush. The process that converts soybeans into oil and meal.

Crush spread. A futures spread that is long soybeans and short the products oil and meal.

Glossary

Current delivery (month). The futures contract that will come to maturity and become deliverable during the current month; also called spot month.

Day order. An order in effect for only the specified day that becomes void if it has not been executed by the close of that day's session.

Day trader. A commodity trader who takes a position in the futures markets and offsets the position in the same trading session.

Default. (1) In reference to the federal farm loan program, the decision on the part of a producer of commodities not to repay the government loan but instead to surrender his crops; (2) in futures markets, the theoretical failure of a party to a futures contract to either make or take delivery of the physical commodity as required under the contract.

Deferred contracts. Contracts that will mature after the current (spot) delivery month. Also call distant or back contracts.

Deferred delivery. (1) Synonymous with forward contracting; (2) the most distant months in which futures trading is taking place, as distinguished from the nearby futures delivery months.

Deliverable grades. See Contract grades.

Delivery notice. Notice from the clearing house of a seller's intention to deliver the physical commodity against his or her short futures position; precedes and is distinct from the warehouse receipt or shipping certificate, which is the instrument of transfer of ownership.

Delivery points. Those locations designated by commodity exchanges at which stocks of a commodity represented by a futures contract may be delivered in fulfillment of the contract.

Delivery price. The official settlement price of the trading session during which the buyer of futures contracts receives through the clearinghouse a notice of the seller's intention to deliver, at the price at which the buyer must pay for commodities represented by the futures contract.

Differentials. Price differences between classes, grades, and locations of different stocks of the same commodity.

Discount. (1) A downward adjustment in price allowed for delivery of stocks of a commodity of less than deliverable grade against a futures contract; (2) sometimes used to refer to the price differences between futures of different delivery months, as in the phrase "July at a discount to May," indicating that the price of the July future is lower than that of the May.

Discretionary account. An arrangement by which the holder of the account gives written power of attorney to another, often a broker, to make buying and selling decisions without notification to the holder; often referred to as the managed account or the controlled account.

Dominant futures. The futures contract having the largest number of open contracts (largest open interest).

Econometrics. The use of statistical and mathematical methods in the field of economics to verify and develop economic theories.

Elasticity. A characteristic of a commodity that describes the interaction of supply, demand, and price of a commodity; *demand elasticity*—a commodity is said to be elastic in demand when a price change creates an increase or a decrease in consumption; *supply elasticity*—the supply of a commodity is said to be elastic when a change in price creates a change in the production of the commodity; *inelasticity* of supply or of demand exists in either of the reverse situations, when either supply or demand is relatively unresponsive to changes in price.

Evening up. The act of covering or liquidating futures contract so that a spread exists or there is no net position.

FCM. Futures Commission Merchant.

FINEX. Financial Instrument Exchange (division of the New York Cotton Exchange), 4 World Trade Center,

New York, NY 10048, Phone (212) 938-2634, Fax (212) 432-0294.

F.O.B. Free on board; indicates that all delivery, inspection, and elevation or loading costs involved in putting commodities on board a carrier have been paid.

FOK. Fill or kill, a term used with a futures order meaning the order has to be filled immediately at the price specified or the order is to be killed, that is, made invalid.

Feed ratios. The variable relationships of the cost of feeding animals to market weight sales prices, expressed as ratios, such as the hog/corn ratio. These serve as indicators of the profit or lack of it in feeding animals to market weight.

First notice day. First day on which notices of intention to deliver cash commodities against futures contracts can be presented by sellers and received by buyers through the exchange clearinghouse.

Floor broker. An exchange member or a representative of an exchange member who executes orders on behalf of his or her clients or firm.

Foreign material. An unacceptable material found in a commodity during the course of inspection; material that must be removed from a commodity before it can be sold or the price must be discounted.

Glossary

Forward contracting. A cash transaction common in many industries, including commodity merchandising, in which the buyer and seller agree upon delivery of a specified quality and quantity of goods at a specified future date. A specific price may be agreed upon in advance, or there may be an agreement that the price will be determined at the time of delivery on the basis of either the prevailing local cash price or a futures price.

Free supply. Stocks of a commodity which are available for commercial sale, as distinguished from government-owned or government-controlled stocks.

Full carrying charge. See Carrying charges (or costs).

Fundamental analysis. An approach to analysis of futures markets and commodity futures price trends which examines the underlying factors that will affect the supply and demand of the commodity being traded in futures contracts. See also Sentiment analysis and Technical analysis.

Fundamentalist. A trader or market analyst who bases his or her evaluation of future commodity prices on fundamental analysis. See also Fundamental analysis.

Fungibility. The characteristic of total interchangeability. Futures contracts for the same commodity and delivery month are fungible because of their standardized specifications for quality, quantity, delivery date, and delivery locations.

Futures. Legally binding contracts involving the purchase and sale of commodities, and so on, for delivery at a specified time and place at a future date and in accordance with the rules and regulations of the exchange where they are traded.

Futures commission merchant. An individual or organization that solicits or accepts orders to buy or sell futures contracts or commodity options and accepts money or other assets from customers in connection with such orders. An FCM must be registered with the CFTC.

GTC. Good Till Canceled, a term used with a futures order meaning the order is to remain open until it has been executed or canceled by the originator.

Grain Futures Act. Federal statute which regulates trading in grain futures, effective June 22, 1923; administered by the U.S. Department of Agriculture; amended in 1936, creating the Commodity Exchange Authority, and since referred to as the Commodity Exchange Act.

Grain Processing Margin (GPM). The difference between the cost of soybeans and the combined sales income of the soybean oil and meal which results from processing soybeans. Other industries have similar formulas to express the relationship of raw material costs to sales income from finished products.

Hedger. A person or company that deals in a commodity, either as producer or processor, and wants to minimize the financial risk involved. See also Hedging.

Glossary

Hedging. A means of protecting against prices changes in commodities or securities. In the futures markets, price protection is typically accomplished by the sale of futures contracts in anticipation of sales of cash commodities at some future date. Thus, a decline in prices in the futures markets will be offset by a rise in the cash price when the two transactions are consummated, or vice versa. See also Buying hedge and Selling hedge.

High. The highest cash or futures price recorded during a given time period, for example, a trading session, a week, or a month.

IMM. International Monetary Market (division of the Chicago Mercantile Exchange), 30 South Wacker Drive, Chicago, IL 60606, Phone (312) 930-1000, Fax (312) 930-3439.

IOM. Index and Option Market (division of the Chicago Mercantile Exchange), 30 South Wacker Drive, Chicago, IL 60606, Phone (312) 930-1000, Fax (312) 930-3439.

Initial margin. The amount of money a customer must deposit with his or her broker prior to placing an order with the broker for a futures contract or contracts. The required deposit varies with the brokerage firm but is typically somewhat more than the minimum margin requirement set by the exchanges. It is usually 5 to 10 percent of the value of the contract. See also Maintenance margin.

Glossary

Intercommodity spread. A spread involving two different but related commodities, for example, long October Cattle versus short October Hogs.

Intercrop spread. A spread involving a single commodity but contract months in different crop years, for example, long July Soybeans versus short November Soybeans.

Intergrain spread. An intercommodity spread in the grains—that is, a spread involving two different but related commodities, for example, long July Wheat versus short July Corn.

Intermarket spread. A spread involving two different exchanges, for example, long Kansas City July Wheat versus short Chicago July Wheat.

Introducing broker. A firm or individual that solicits and accepts commodity futures orders from customers but does not accept money, securities, or property from the customer. An IB must be registered with the CFTC and must carry all accounts through an FCM on a fully disclosed basis.

Inverted market. A futures market in which the nearer months are selling at a premium over the more distant months; characteristically, a market in which there is a shortage of current supplies.

Invisible supply. Uncounted stocks of a commodity in the hands of wholesalers, manufactures, and producers which cannot be identified accurately; stocks outside commercial channels but theoretically available to the market.

Job lot. A quantity of a commodity less than the quantity specified in the corresponding futures contract.

KCBT. Kansas City Board of Trade, 4800 Main Street, Suite 303, Kansas City, MO 64112, Phone (816) 753-7500, Fax (816) 753-3944.

Key reversal day. A day during which the range of prices and the closing price indicate that a top in the market has occurred and subsequent prices are likely to decline. A term used and defined in text dealing with technical analysis.

Last trading day. Day on which trading ceases in the contract for the maturing (current) delivery month.

Leg. One of the positions in a spread, either long or short, such as the short leg of the spread is in the November contract.

Leverage. A financial advantage in which a small amount of money can control a large amount of money or something of large value, for example, in the futures market, it only requires an initial margin deposit of 5 to 10 percent of the value of a commodity for control. Thus, a small rise or decline in the value of a commodity can result in a substantial profit or loss to a futures trader.

Life of contract. Period between the beginning of trading in a particular futures contract and the expiration of trading (last trading day).

Limit down. The maximum price decline from the previous day's settlement price permitted for a commodity in one trading session by the rules of the exchange.

Limit only. A term relating to an order that restricts its execution to buy for not more than or to sell for not less than the stated price.

Limit order. An order in which the customer sets a limit on either price or time of execution, or both.

Limit up. The maximum price advance from the previous day's settlement price permitted for a commodity in one trading session by the rules of the exchange.

Liquid market. A market where selling and buying can be accomplished with ease, owing to the presence of a large number of interested buyers and sellers.

Liquidation. The sale of futures contracts to offset the obligation to take delivery of an equal number of futures contracts of the same delivery month purchased earlier.

Loan price. The government-established price of a commodity which determines the amount of money a producer may borrow who has signed up for that commodity program. At harvest time producers can accept the loan price for their crops or they can sell their crops on the free market and repay the government loan.

Loan program. Primary means of government agricultural price support operations in which the government lends money to farmers at preannounced rates, with the farmers' crops used as collateral. Default on these loans is the primary method by which the government acquires stocks of agricultural commodities.

Long. One who has bought a cash commodity or a commodity futures contract, in contrast to a short, who has sold a cash commodity or futures contract. Opposite of short.

Long the basis. One who has bought (long) the cash (actual) commodity.

Low. The lowest cash or futures price recorded during a given time period, for example, a trading session, a week, a month.

Midam. Midamerica Commodity Exchange, 141 West Jackson Boulevard, Chicago, IL 60604, Phone (312) 341-3000, Fax (312) 341-3027.

MIT. Term meaning "market if touched." An MIT order becomes a market order if a specific price is touched during trading.

Maintenance margin. For open positions, the minimum amount of money per commodity per contract that a customer must maintain in the account at all times to protect the broker against losses.

Maintenance margin call.   See margin call.

Managed account.   An arrangement by which the holder of the account gives written power of attorney to another, often his or her broker, to make buying and selling decisions without notification to the holder; also referred to as the discretionary account or the controlled account.

Margin.   See Initial margin and Maintenance margin.

Margin call.   A call from a broker to a customer to deposit additional money in the account to cover losses and bring the margin back up to the maintenance margin level.

Market composition.   The distribution of hedgers (also frequently referred to as the commercials), large speculators, small speculators, and speculators who are spread in the market. The long and short distribution is typically expressed in the number of contracts held by each group or as a percentage of the total outstanding contracts.

Market order.   An order to immediately buy at the lowest asking price when the order is received in the trading pit, or conversely, an order to sell at the highest bid price.

Glossary

Marketing quota. A federal government restriction limiting the amount of a particular commodity that farmers may sell or grow on their allocated acreage.

Maturity. A period of time during which a futures contract can be settled by delivery of the actual commodity; the period between the first notice day and the last trading day of a commodity futures contract.

Member's commission. Commission charged for executing an order for a person who is a member of the exchange.

Member's rate. Same as Member's commission.

Moving average. A term used by technical analysts to refer to the average price calculated each day for the past number of X days. Typically, the closing price is used. For example, a 12-day moving average would be calculated each day using the closing price for the prior 12 days. A moving average is generally used to reveal the market trend.

NYCE. New York Cotton Exchange, 4 World Trade Center, New York, NY 10048, Phone (212) 938-2702, Fax (212) 488-8135.

NYFE. New York Futures Exchange, 20 Broad Street, New York, NY 10005, Phone 656-4949, Fax (212) 656-2925.

NYMEX. New York Mercantile Exchange, 4 World Trade Center, New York, NY 10048, Phone (212) 938-2222, Fax (212) 938-2985.

National Futures Association. 200 W. Madison St., Suite 1600, Chicago, IL 60606, Phone (312) 781-1300, Fax (312) 781-1467, (800) 621-3570. The NFA is the congressionally authorized self-regulatory organization of the futures industry in the United States. It began operations on October 1, 1982, and over the years has taken over many of the registration and disciplinary responsibilities of the CFTC.

Nearby. The futures contract nearest to maturity. Sometimes referred to as the nearby month or nearby delivery.

Net position. The difference between the number of long and short positions held in a given commodity. Positions held may be in different contract months.

New crop. The crop that has yet to mature and be harvested.

Nominal price. Declared price for a futures month when recent trading has not taken place. Typically, the price midway between the bid and asked prices.

Notice day. See First notice day.

Notice of delivery. See Delivery notice.

Glossary

OCO. Term meaning "one cancels other." Used when two orders have been entered by a trader who wants to cancel one order if the other is executed.

Offer. A price at which a trader is willing to sell.

Offset. Closing out futures positions by taking offsetting positions, either long or short, to positions previously held.

Old crop. The most recently harvested crop that is being distributed or stored.

Omnibus account. An account in which the activity of two or more traders are commingled and the identity of the traders is not disclosed. Forbidden by some brokerage firms and illegal on some exchanges.

On track. A type of deferred delivery in which the price is set F.O.B. seller's location and the buyer agrees to pay freight cost to his destination. Sometimes referred to as track country station.

On the close. The time during a trading session when an order is to be executed, in this case, within about a minute prior to the close of a given trading session. Some brokerage firms will not accept this type of order since its execution cannot be guaranteed.

On the open. The time during a trading session when an order is to be executed, in this case when a given trading session begins.

Glossary

Open contracts.   Futures contracts that represent a position in the market.

Open interest.   The number of outstanding futures contracts in a given contract month for a specific commodity at the close of a given trading session. Since there must be a long contract for every short contract, and vice versa, one long contract and one short contract represent an open interest of one. Open interest does not include open futures contracts against which notices of delivery have been issued by the clearing organization of an exchange.

Open order.   A valid order that has yet to be executed and remains on the brokers' books until canceled.

Opening bell.   A bell used by some exchanges to signal the opening of a given trading session.

Open outcry.   Verbal method of declaring bids and offers in the trading pits or rings of commodity exchanges. Though the expression is inaccurate, it also refers to bids and offers made via hand signals.

Opening price.   The price, or range of prices, recorded during the time period designated by the exchange as the official opening of a given trading session.

Opening range.   Range of closely related prices at which transactions took place within the first few seconds after a given trading session opened.

Option. The right to buy (a call option) or to sell (a put option) a futures contract at a specified price within a given period of time. Options are also available for stocks and other financial instruments.

Original margin. The initial amount of money a customer must deposit with his or her broker prior to initiating futures trading. The minimum margin per commodity per contract is determined by the exchange; typically, the margin set by the broker is somewhat higher.

Overbought. A market condition, following a sharp rise in prices due to heavy buying, which now lacks sufficient buyers to move the market higher. The situation is also referred to as a contrary opinion situation if the market is severely overbought. A sharp decline in prices typically occurs when the market becomes overbought because there are insufficient buyers left or all of the buyers have already bought.

Oversold. A market condition, following a sharp decline in prices due to heavy selling, which now lacks sufficient sellers to drive the market lower. The situation is also referred to as a contrary opinion situation if the market is severely oversold. A sharp rise in prices typically occurs when the market becomes oversold because there are insufficient sellers left or all of the sellers have already sold.

P & S or P & L. Purchase and sale statement or profit and loss statement. A statement of transactions provided by brokerage firms to customers showing dates, prices, profits or losses, number of contracts, commission charges, and so forth.

Paper losses. Losses on actual open futures positions; not related to paper trading.

Paper profits. Profits on actual open futures positions; not related to paper trading.

Paper trading. Simulated futures trading using the same steps as if one were actually trading. All steps are recorded on paper to determine approximately how one would have fared in actual trading.

Parity. An artificial price of an agricultural commodity established by the government to offset inflation factors involved in producing the commodity; thus, a unit of the commodity represents a constant purchasing power for the producer.

Pit. The area in the exchange where futures trading of a commodity takes place, generally just a single commodity. The pit configuration varies among exchanges; in the Chicago Board of Trade, for example, the pit is octagonal with steps descending to center; the steps are in so-called rings. Each ring is devoted to transactions involving a specific contract month or group of months.

Point. The minimum price move in a specific commodity that is allowed by the exchange.

Glossary

Pool operators.   See Commodity pool operator.

Position.   A trader's commitment to being either long or short in the market. Sometimes used incorrectly and interchangeably to mean a futures contract.

Position limit.   The maximum number of futures contracts that the Commodity Futures Trading Commission allows one trader to hold in a given commodity.

Position trader.   One who enters either the long or the short side of the market and anticipates maintaining the position for an extended period of time, for example, several months.

Posture.   How one is positioned in the market, either short or long.

Premium.   (1) The price difference between two different contract months of the same futures—that is, one contract month is said to be trading at a premium to another contract month; (2) the additional price allowed by exchange regulations for a commodity meeting higher-than-required standards or grades.

Price averaging.   A procedure used to buy or sell a number of futures contracts over a period of time such that the average price of all positions is reasonable.

Price limit.   For a given trading session in a specific futures, the maximum price advance or decline from

179

the prior day's settlement price that is allowed by the exchange.

Primary market. The location where major producers of a specific commodity bring the commodity for sale, for example, a primary market in commodity X might be Kansas City, Missouri.

Professional speculator. A person who makes his or her primary living by speculating in the futures markets.

Program trading. A trading method wherein entries and exits to a market are made at predetermined prices and/or conditions, typically implemented by a computer.

Public elevators. State and federal licensed and regulated grain storage facilities which, in some cases, are approved as a depository of commodities against futures contracts.

Purchase agreement. An agreement between the government and a producer to buy the producer's product at a specified time for the government's loan value.

Put. A term applied to an option to sell a futures contract or other security at a specified price within a given time period.

Pyramiding. The act of using paper profits from earlier transactions to buy or sell a decreasing number of futures contracts over a period of time such that the number of positions forms an approximate pyramid (equilateral triangle). Inverse pyramiding, which is considered highly risky, is an act wherein an increasing number of contracts are bought or sold over a period of time with paper profits.

RIA.   Registered Investment advisor

Range.   The difference between the highest and lowest prices encountered during a given time period, for example, a trading session, a week, a month.

Reaction.   A sharp price decline following a significant advance; the inverse of a recovery.

Realized profits.   Actual profits resulting from closing out market positions.

Recovery.   A sharp price advance following a significant decline; the inverse of a reaction.

Registered commodity representative.   Someone who is registered with an exchange to solicit and handle commodity customer business for his or her firm.

Registered Investment Advisor (RIA)   Someone who is registered with the Securities and Exchange Commission to handle securities business as well as futures.

Regularity.   A term related to a processing plant or warehouse that meets exchange requirements and is approved to accept delivery of commodities against futures contracts.

Regulated commodity. A commodity regulated by the Commodity Futures Trading Commission.

Reportable positions. An ambiguous term used by the CFTC in which positions means contracts. See also Reporting level.

Reporting level. The number of futures contracts in anyone's holdings which, if exceeded, must be reported each day to the CFTC. The report must specify the number of contracts, the contract months, and whether the holder of those contracts is speculating or hedging. There is no reporting requirement when the number of contracts held is less than the reporting level.

Resistance. A price level above current prices which is expected to provide resistance and limit any further advance in prices.

Resting order. An open order that is unlikely to be filled immediately, that is, an order that is outside the present range of prices but may be executable in the near future.

Retender. The right of a holder of a long futures contract who has been tendered a delivery notice to offer (retender) the notice to another party. Relieves the holder of a long contract from taking delivery of the commodity. Retendering is applicable only to certain commodities and within a specified period of time.

Reverse crush spread.   A spread involving the purchase of soybean oil and soybean meal contracts against the sale of soybean contracts.

Ring.   See Pit.

Rolling forward.   The act of exiting from a position in an expiring contract month and taking an equivalent position in a more distant contract month.

Rolling over.   See Rolling forward.

Round lot.   A quantity of a commodity equal to the quantity specified in the corresponding futures contract.

Round turn.   The act of taking a position and later closing out the position in the futures market; a round trip is a simile.

Sample grade.   Typically, the lowest quality of a commodity acceptable for delivery against a futures contract.

Sampling.   A sample quantity of a commodity taken by an inspector for the purpose of grading it.

Scalper.   Typically, a speculator on the floor of an exchange who is willing to buy and sell futures contracts for very small potential profits. Usually, a scalper is willing to buy slightly below or sell slightly above the last transaction and thus makes many trades during a given session. Scalpers provide much of a market's liquidity.

Scalping.   The act of buying and selling futures contracts for very small potential profits.

Selling hedge (or short hedge).   Selling futures contracts to protect against a possible decline in the price of the commodity at some specific date in the future. See also Hedging.

Sell on opening or close.   To sell at the beginning or as the trading session ends at a price within the closing or opening range of prices.

Sell on stop.   A market order to sell when and if prices decline and touch a specified price. Order is used principally as a stop loss order for a long position or to enter the market on the short side when and if prices break out on the downside below a support level.

Sentiment analysis.   A system of market analysis based on the sentiment (bullish, neutral, or bearish) of traders in a specific market as opposed to fundamental or technical analysis.

Settlement price.   An official price established by the exchange after the close of a trading session for the purpose of clearing all transactions. The settlement price may differ, usually only by a small amount from the price of the last reported trade. Trading immediately before the close can involve a range of prices which are roughly averaged to determine the settlement price.

Glossary

Short. One who has sold a cash commodity that has not been delivered or sold futures contracts. Opposite of long.

Short covering. The purchase of futures contracts to cover an earlier sale of an equal number of contacts of the same delivery month.

Short hedge. The act of selling futures contracts to guard against losses or to protect profits in a cash commodity that is on hand or will be delivered after harvest.

Short squeeze. A situation wherein the deliverable supplies of a given commodity against a futures contract are in short supply. The shorts are being squeezed, since they can't deliver the commodity, and must cover their positions by buying futures contracts. Prices are being inflated by the longs whose continued buying is driving prices higher.

Soil bank. A federal government program that pays commodity producers to let a portion of their land remain idle. The object is to reduce production so that prices can be maintained at a predetermined level.

Speculator. One whose primary interest is buying and selling for short-term profits (typically, a period of a few months or less) and has no interest in the production or processing of a commodity.

Glossary

Spot commodity. The actual commodity as traded in the cash markets.

Spot month. The earliest deliverable futures contract month. Also frequently referred to as the nearby month.

Spot price. The price of the cash commodity.

Spread. A position in which the speculator is long in one contract month and is short a corresponding number of contracts in another contract month. Also occasionally referred to as a straddle.

Stop loss order. See Stop order.

Stop order. A market order to buy (at the market) when and if prices rise and touch a specified price or conversely. Also referred to as a stop loss order when used to protect an open position. An order whose execution will (1) tend to provide protection against losses or the reduction of profits as a result of an unfavorable price movement, or (2) provide an entry to the market in the event of a price breakout; short if the breakout is on the downside, long if the breakout is on the upside.

Straddle. Has the same meaning as spread. See Spread.

Strong hands. The hedgers (commercials) and well-financed professional speculators who are relatively immune to price moves that would typically cause other traders to exit the market either voluntarily or involuntarily.

Support. A price level below current prices which is expected to provide support and limit any further decline in prices.

Switch. An act employed to maintain a position in a commodity when the position held is in the expiring contract month; the position in the expiring contract month is liquidated or covered, and a corresponding position is taken in a farther out contract month.

TCBT. Twin Cities Board of Trade, 430 First Avenue North, Minneapolis, MN 55401, Phone (612) 333-6742, Fax (612) 333-8728.

Tax spread. Now an illegal means (used in the past when it was legal) for converting short-term profits into a long-term capital gain, or for shifting income from a high-tax year into a more favorable future year.

Technical analysis. A system of market analysis based on market parameters as opposed to analysis based on the underlying fundamentals that determine supply and demand. Market parameters include price, volume, open interest, market sentiment, and market composition.

Technical correction. A minor retracing of a significant rise or decline in prices which cannot be attributed to a change in the fundamentals.

Technical rally (or decline). A price move attributable to technical factors rather than any underlying fundamentals.

Tender. A delivery notice, usually in the form of a warehouse receipt, confirming that a party who is short in the market has made delivery of the commodity in accordance with the terms of the futures contract. The notice is provided to the clearing house, which in turn passes the notice to the oldest buyer of record in that delivery month of the commodity.

Terminal elevator. A major grain storage facility at key marketing centers in the United States.

To-arrive contract. A contract in which the price of the commodity is based on delivery to a designated point with the seller paying the shipping costs.

Trading limit. (1) The limit on the *trading* range in one trading session which is set by the rules of the exchange; (2) also the maximum number of contracts that a trader may hold, net long or short, at any time.

Trading range. See Range.

Transfer notice. See Delivery notice.

Transferable notice. See Retender.

Trend. The general direction (up, down, or sideways) of prices for a given commodity or index.

USDA. United States Department of Agriculture.

USDC. United States Department of Commerce.

USDL. United States Department of Labor.

Unwinding. Liquidation of a spread.

Variation margin. A term having the same meaning as maintenance margin. See Maintenance margin.

Variation margin call. A term having the same meaning as maintenance margin call. See Maintenance margin call.

Visible supply. The amount of the actual commodity known to exist in elevators or warehouses at any particular time.

Volume. The number of contracts of a specific commodity traded during a given period, for example, a trading session, a week, or a month. Inasmuch as there is a long for every short contract and vice versa, a volume of one is the purchase of one contract and the sale of one contract.

Warehouse receipt. A document guaranteeing the existence and availability of a given quantity and quality of a commodity in storage; typically used as an instrument to transfer ownership of a commodity in storage.

Wash sale. An illegal and fictitious transaction for tax purposes involving the simultaneous purchase and sale of futures contracts; profits are transferred from person A to B, while the corresponding loss is transferred from person B to A.

Weak hands. Traders who hold only a few futures contracts and are considered to have little staying power in the market because of their apparent limited finances.

Weather market. A market in which the weather is affecting commodity prices because of growing or harvesting conditions and so on.

Widening. A spread in which the distant contract month is gaining on the nearby month.

Wire services. An old term referring to the distribution of commodity data and information via wire.

INDEX

Index

Index

Index